Rivals! A confrontation in Lancashire as a steam tram of Heywood Corporation meets an electric car of Rochdale Corporation at the municipal boundary. The date is 1905, and the steamer is making one of its last journeys before yielding to the all-conquering electric tram.

TRAMS OF THE PAST

Photographs from the Whitcombe Collection

Edited by J. Joyce

LONDON

IAN ALLAN LTD

First published 1979

ISBN 0 7110 0923 6

Published by Ian Allan Ltd, Shepperton, Surrey; and printed in the United Kingdom by Ian Allan Printing Ltd

Contents

Introduction

The name of Dr H. A. Whitcombe has long been known to the transport historian, and photographs credited to the Whitcombe Collection have graced specialised publications on tramway history. Up to now, however, the full scope of the Collection has remained largely unrealised, with many of the pictures rarely if ever seeing the light of day. The publishers have therefore thought it worthwhile to bring the Collection to the notice of the growing numbers of those interested in transport history by offering a selection of the photographs in the present volume. Inevitably this can include only a fraction of the total of around 10,000 photographs, but at least it yields a hint of the treasures to be discovered there. It is believed that the majority of the illustrations will be unfamiliar to most of today's enthusiasts, and that they will reveal a fresh portrait of the trams of the past.

In its range the Collection amounts in effect to a history of tramways from their origins to the years of their heyday and the brink of their decline. We see the horse cars at work in the streets of the bustling Victorian towns; the development of mechanical traction with the steam tram, cable haulage and other forms of power such as gas and petrol engines; then the transformation brought about by the appearance of the electric cars, which inaugurated a new era in local transport with fast, clean and cheap travel. From its beginnings the tram spread around the world until almost every self-respecting city and town boasted tracks in its main thoroughfares.

All these phases in the story are represented in the Collection by photographs from a multitude of sources; there are makers' photographs proudly recording the latest products to emerge from their works; commercial view cards of local scenery, with the new trams prominently in sight; cumbersome glass plates on which enterprising photographers froze the events of their home towns. The pictures provide us with a panorama of social history, as well as an insight into the day-to-day operation of a great industry serving the needs of the busy towns. We observe the trams in action, visit the depots and the stables where the tram horses lived, watch the steam trams taking on their fuel and water, meet the men who tended them, and admire the pristine electric cars as they glide out along their newly laid tracks.

Nor was Dr Whitcombe's interest confined to the urban landscape of Britain; here also is the wider world beyond the seas. We observe the indomitable steam trams of the Low Countries negotiating the Flemish fields and the Dutch polders, enduring surprisingly late along the neat roadsides and in the narrow village streets. Far across the world we travel to South Africa and the dusty streets of India, then to the Dutch East Indies and Burma. Continuing to Australia and New Zealand, we find trams in some ways so like those of Britain, but in other ways so different.

Yet undoubtedly the most fascinating pictures of all are those depicting the industrial towns of Britain, for Dr Whitcombe himself took up his camera to capture for us a unique series of scenes from British tramways during the late 1920s. At this date there were few amateur photographers of town transport — the day of the bus spotter had not yet dawned — so these are an unrivalled record of an era that was rapidly fading, for the trams were then reaching the end of their days of glory. Now not only have the trams gone; the entire scene has been transformed, since many of these streets have vanished with the demolition of the apparently solid and immutable structures of the Industrial Revolution — the towering mills and the long rows of terrace houses. Thus the pictures have a value not only to the transport enthusiast, but to the industrial archaeologist and the social historian. While a few of these photographs have been reproduced elsewhere, this is the first time that a major selection has been published in collected form.

Creator of the Collection, Harold Arthur Whitcombe was a member of the medical profession; Bachelor of Medicine in 1910, he became a Fellow of the Royal Society of Medicine and a Fellow of the Royal Institute of Public Health. He also served as a Lieutenant in the Royal Army Medical Corps. His other interests are reflected in his Fellowship of the Society of Genealogists and his contribution on the Whitcombe family to the *Pedigree Register*. His life-long interest in tramways seems to have originated during his boyhood in his native Birmingham in the 1890s when, as he tells us, he used to travel daily to and from school by steam tram, 'often, it must be confessed, on the footplate, squatting hidden behind the coke bunker!' The steam tram remained his especial favourite, and his monograph on the *History of the Steam Tram* has become a classic of transport literature; 'most doctors love engines', he said, perhaps because 'there is nothing so nearly living as the steam locomotive' — a sentiment that will strike an answering chord in the heart of many an enthusiast. Through his generosity, his vast collection of photographs passed into the safe keeping of the Science Museum in London after his death in 1943, thus preserving for the future this fine store of pictures of trams of the past.

As well as bringing to the general view something of the richness of the Whitcombe Collection, it is hoped that this book will serve as a modest tribute to the memory of an enthusiast to whom later enthusiasts are greatly indebted.

Acknowledgements

Thanks are due to Mr Ian Allan for initiating the idea of this book; to Mr John Parke, Editor of *Buses*, for suggestions on the content and format; to the Director of the Science Museum for allowing the use of the Collection; and in particular to Mr P. D. Stephens, until recently Assistant Keeper, Rail Transport Collection, Science Museum, his assistant Mr B. C. Ironmonger, and the staff of the Museum's photographic studio, for their very considerable aid and patience during the process of selecting the photographs and preparing the required prints.

PART 1

In the Tramway Age

The tram at the peak of its glory; a product of the technology of its time, the tramway introduced a new mobility to the growing cities and towns of an increasingly urbanised world. It harnessed both the engineering skill and the capital of an advancing society to create a new industry that stood well in the forefront of progress. The horse car established itself during the 1860s and 1870s, but its high costs and limited power led to the quest for a motive force that could provide higher speed and greater efficiency.

Mechanical traction came in the form of the steam tram, which enjoyed a fairly brief heyday during the 1880s and 1890s. Cable operation also had its successes at the same time, while trials were made with gas and oil fuel. But it was electric traction that brought the great tramway boom of the early years of the century; making rapid progress during the 1890s, the electric car went on to supersede horse, steam and cable. The photograph above exemplifies the changeover, as an Edinburgh electric tram stands alongside one of the cable cars it was in the process of replacing.

The photographs in the first half of this volume illustrate something of the tram's progression from its start to its heyday. They suggest not only its variety, but its ubiquity — for truly the tramway was a worldwide institution.

The Tramcar Comes

Above left: 'Street railways' are recorded in some American cities, including New York and New Orleans, during the 1830s. This early New York horse car still shows its omnibus influence in the raised driver's seat and the curved sides. A somewhat similar vehicle was running a service on a dock railway in Liverpool in 1859, while Paris had started its first trams in 1853. **Left:** A Liverpool car of 1869, though built in England at the Birkenhead works of George Starbuck, is typically American in design. **Above:** The opening of Britain's first 'street railway' in Birkenhead in 1860. It was promoted by an American, George Francis Train, who also introduced three short-lived tramways into London in 1861. The Birkenhead tramway survived (there were trams in the town until 1937) and, in spite of some road users who objected to the rails as a danger, other towns became interested in the idea, especially after construction was facilitated by the Tramways Act of 1870. By 1878 Britain had 270 miles of tramways, worked by over 1,000 cars and more than 9,000 horses. **Right:** Sights such as this scene at Neath in South Wales became common in urban areas.

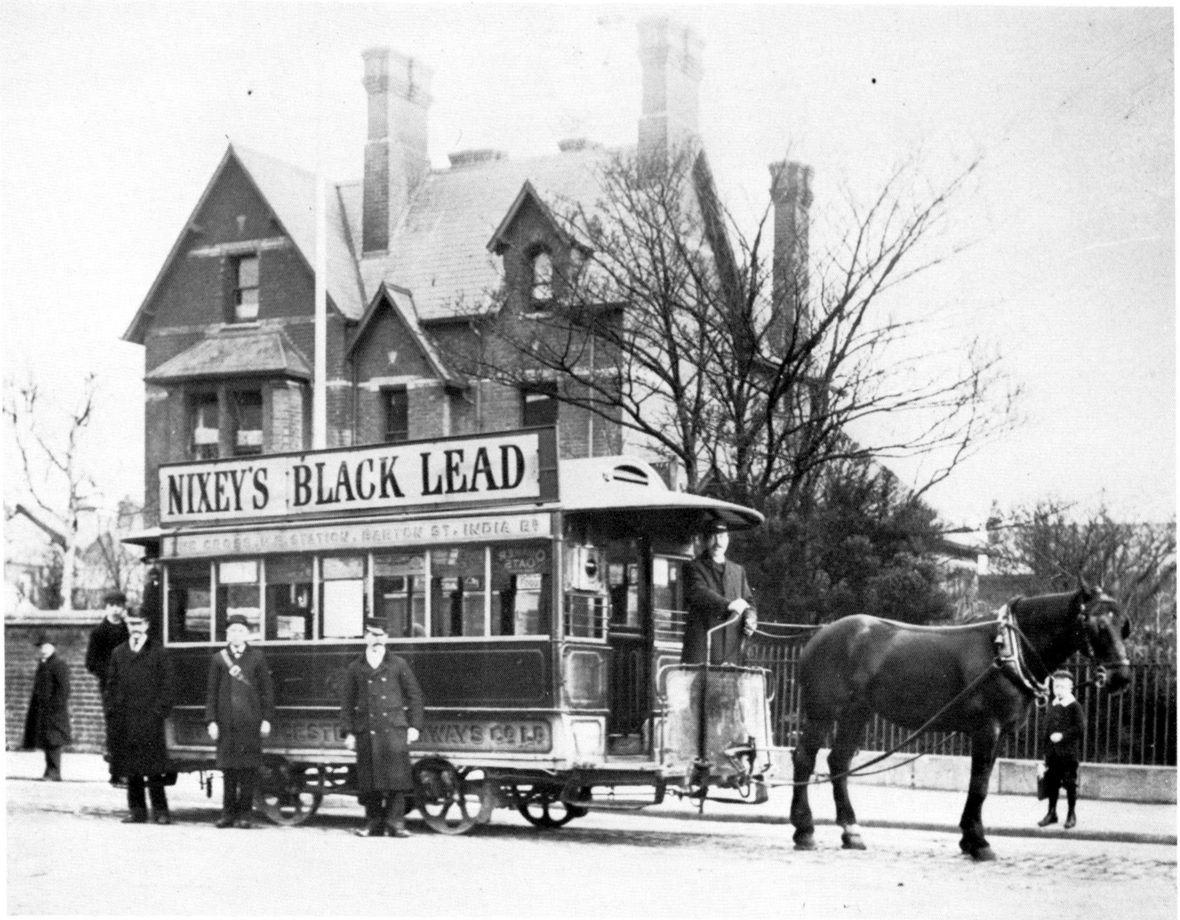
NIXEY'S BLACK LEAD

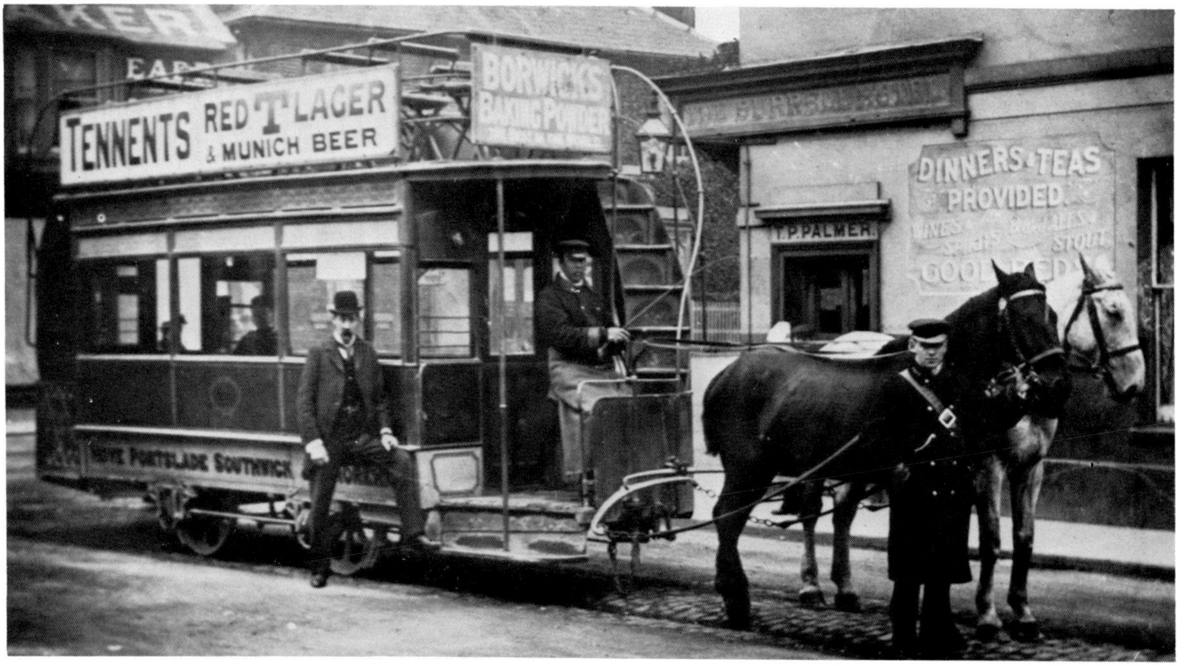
TENNENTS RED T LAGER
& MUNICH BEER
BORWICK'S
BAKING POWDER
DINNERS & TEAS
PROVIDED
T.P. PALMER
HOVE PORTSLADE SOUTHWICK

Some varieties of horse trams posed with their crews. **Above left:** A one-horse single-decker suitable for lightly loaded routes. This one is in Gloucester. A typical one-horse car weighed little more than one ton and carried 14-16 passengers. **Left:** A two-horse double decker with 'garden seats' on the upper deck, on the Brighton and Shoreham tramway. Such a vehicle weighed about $2\frac{1}{2}$ tons and carried 46 passengers. **Above:** Another two-horse double-decker, this time an earlier design with 'knifeboard' upper-deck seating, in Dundee. **Right:** On the Manchester Tramways and Carriage Company, a reversible car of Eades patent of 1877; to save unhitching the horses, the single-ended body was made to swivel on its underframe.

Above: A glimpse of trams in Continental European countries. Germany had street tramways in the 1860s. In Düsseldorf the first line was opened in 1876, and here is a typical one-horse car of the Rheinische Bahngesellschaft; it accommodated 12 seated passengers and 12 standing. **Centre right:** In Holland, another one-horse car, this time in Rotterdam where the first trams started in 1879. The Rotterdam Electric Tramways Company (RETM) was formed in 1904 to take over the earlier company and electrify the lines. **Bottom right:** After trials with the double-deck 'Imperial', Continental operators generally found the smaller one-horse vehicle a more practical proposition. This car served the Dutch town of 's Graveland.

Horse Car Days

Above: This idyllic scene at The Swan on Clapton Common about 1890 is a reminder that the suburban terminus could still appear almost rural in horse car days. The new trams helped to give city-dwellers easy access to the country. London had some 60 miles of tramways in 1876 and 130 miles in 1891. **Left:** In the busy towns, the tracks soon became an accepted part of the street. This view of South Shields about 1900 shows a two-horse double-decker; in the distance can be seen its rival, the horse omnibus.

Above left: Boarding the car; a New York street scene of the 1890s. Horse cars generally stopped anywhere on request to pick up or set down, though the more energetic passenger was not expected to wait until the tram had come to a halt! **Left:** Steep hills called for the services of a third horse — the trace horse. Even so, life for the animals was hard; tramway expert D. K. Clark wrote in 1878: 'The employment of horse-power in the dire work of starting and dragging the ponderous cars is an element of barbarism.' The car shown here is another Eades reversible, this time on the Bolton and District Tramways, which began services in 1880. **Above:** Emerging from the depot to start the day's work is a car on the Porth-Pontypridd route of the Pontypridd and Rhondda Valley Tramways. **Right:** The horse car at home; this depot view shows single-deck and double-deck cars of the Stockport and Hazel Grove tramway.

The stables — the 'power house' of the horse tramways. The whole operation of the system depended on a good stock of healthy horses. Each car needed at least 11 horses to keep it going: five pairs on duty, plus one spare horse. Although a horse worked only some 15 miles a day, its normal life in tramway service was usually little more than four years. By contrast the men worked 70 or 80 hours a week. These scenes are on the Stockport and Hazel Grove tramway.

Horse cars reach the end of the line. **Top:** New tracks being laid in New York for electric cars. **Above:** Although most horse tramways had succumbed by the early years of the twentieth century, England's last example continued along the sea front at Morecambe until 1926. **Left:** In Wales, the horse tramway between Pwllheli and Llanbedrog ended in 1927 when rough seas washed away part of the track.

Steam in the Streets

'Tramways will not take their fitting place in the system of transport until mechanical power is established in substitution for the power of horses'. Thus wrote D. K. Clark in 1878. The first effective mechanical power was steam. **Above:** England's first steam tram, the Grantham car of 1872, was tried in London and then at Wantage. **Left:** In America, this steam car built by Grice and Long in 1859 was used in Philadelphia. Steam tramway practice generally came to favour the use of a separate locomotive. **Above right:** A pioneer was the 1876 engine of Hughes' design seen here at work on the Vale of Clyde tramways. **Right:** A Green engine and Ashbury car on the Blackburn and Over Darwen tramways. The partial cover on the top deck gave passengers some protection from smoke and soot.

510 GOVAN PHOTOGRAPHIC STUDIO 510
10

8
STEWART & COMPANY
BLACKBURN
BLACKBURN & OVER DARWEN.

G. A. Scheel
Juwelen-Gold-
Silberwaaren-Lager
CASSEL TRAMWAYS COMPANY
CASSEL TRAMWAYS Co LIMITED

GROOTE ARKT
HOUTPOORT
PAVILJOEN
MERRIJWEATHER'S PATENT
TRAMWAIJ MAATSCHAPPIJ

Top left: The first steam tramway in Germany was opened in Kassel in 1877. The Merryweather engines were required to haul three cars up gradients as steep as 1 in 16 on the three-mile route. **Centre left:** Another Merryweather engine, this time on trial in the historic Dutch town of Haarlem. **Bottom left:** A very mixed train hauled by a Green engine gets under way in Valencia on the Tranvias General de Valencia in 1892.

Above: Claimed to be the first steam locomotives built specially for tramway operation, seven engines of this type were supplied by Manning Wardle for the Pernambuco tramways in Brazil between 1867 and 1870. They were basically railway-type locomotives with 0-4-0 wheel arrangement and with saddle tanks, but were enclosed in an all-over cab. Note the 'cow catchers'. **Centre left:** An 1875 fireless steam locomotive, built to the designs of Lamm and Francq and used in Paris. The engine's boiler was three-quarters filled with water, then a supply of steam was taken on from a stationary boiler. The locomotive thus did not carry any fuel or emit any smoke. **Bottom left:** Elaborately lined-out and dignified with the name *Sir Hugh Lowe*, this 1888 Falcon 0-4-2 worked in Johore. Most tram engines were four-wheelers and weighed about 10 tons.

Life on the Steam Trams

A glimpse behind the scenes. **Above:** The maintenance men beside this locomotive boiler give an indication of its size. **Left:** The engine without its jacket on — the small fifth wheel between the coupled wheels drove the speedometer; regulations generally set the maximum speed at 10mph. This is a Falcon engine of the Burnley and District Tramways. **Below:** Crews prepare to take their charges out on the road. This and the upper picture are of the Birmingham tramways. **Above right:** This workaday scene on the Heywood tramways in their last days shows the size and construction of the cars. The typical double-deck car weighed about four tons and carried 60 passengers. **Right:** An impressive line-up on the Birmingham Central Tramways as the staff pose for the photographer in their Sunday best.

Above right: More scenes on the Birmingham tramways, which formed the most extensive steam-worked system in Britain. Here a permanent way 'train' pauses in its duties while the gang line up for the photographer. Note the condensing pipes on the roof of the engine; there were strict regulations about the emission of smoke and steam. The engine is Birmingham and Midland No 21, built by Green in 1886. **Centre right:** Power tools! A special trailer employed for grinding and cleaning the track is powered by steam from the locomotive. Birmingham Central No 10 was one of a batch of engines built by Kitson in 1884-5.

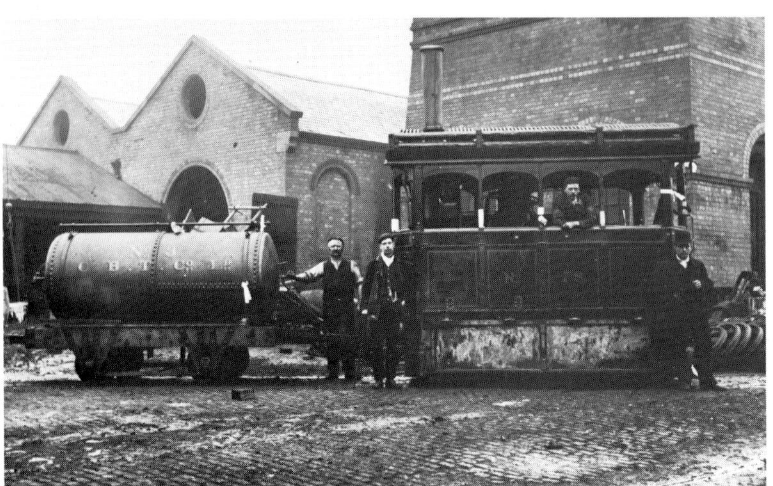

Left: Another item of rolling stock that was not often seen: the gas tank trailer used for the distribution of gas to the depots for car lighting. Gas lighting of tramway cars was considered an advanced feature at the time; most cars had only oil lamps, if they had any interior lighting at all! The engine is City of Birmingham No 78, built by Kitson in the 1890s.

Above: Dr Whitcombe recalled that 'the citizens of Birmingham were proud of their steam trams and acclaimed them before all others for their efficiency, their smooth and silent running and their reliability'. Above is a view of Birmingham in the heyday of steam. **Centre left:** Safety first! A new design of lifeguard is given a practical test in Birmingham. Regulations decreed that the 'works' should be enclosed almost to rail level, hence the box-like outline of the typical tram engine. Dr Whitcombe saw the steam tram as 'something of a hero — martyr perhaps, for it had to combat the unbending prejudice of a public still biased against machinery'. **Bottom left:** Accidents will happen! An embarrassing situation on the Manchester, Bury, Rochdale and Oldham Tramways as the locomotive slews off the track and ends up at right angles to its car. No 70 is a Beyer Peacock engine of Wilkinson design, while the double-deck car is by Starbuck.

Above: Fill her up! A Huddersfield locomotive takes water from a roadside hydrant. This smart turn-out consists of a locomotive by Green and a double-deck car. 'A steam tramway locomotive, when properly cared for, ran smoothly and silently, was free from smell, showed neither steam nor smoke,' wrote Dr Whitcombe. **Right:** These passengers in The Hague seem to be enjoying the ride as they celebrate the Silver Jubilee of their steam tramway in 1912; the locomotive is a Henschel machine of 1890.

Steam Worldwide

Although in Britain the 'train' was usually restricted to only one car, other countries' steam trams were more ambitious. **Above:** A Dutch steam tram in a traditional Dutch setting; a scene on the Demsvaart system in Overijssel. The locomotive is a Henschel of 1916 vintage. Note that while the wheels and motion are covered, it is not enclosed above the footplate. **Below:** In Java, a Beyer Peacock engine at work on the Semarang-Joana tramway, which owned over 200 miles of line. British-built tram engines served in many overseas countries.

The steam tram worldwide. **Left:** In Sydney, Australia; at Deventer in Holland; and at Christchurch, New Zealand. **This page:** At Rangoon in Burma; in Calcutta, India; and in Johore, Malaya.

Above: Dr Whitcombe rejoiced that some countries had escaped the electric mania and kept their steam trams going for many years. Here is a train on the North-South Holland network, seen at Voorburg in 1924; locomotive No 8 was built by Merryweather in 1880. **Centre left:** A train at Takapuna near Auckland in New Zealand, in operation up to 1928. **Bottom left:** In Australia too the steam tram had a lengthy life; this rebuilt Kitson engine was at work in the Sydney suburb of Parramatta, where some services lingered on until 1943. **Above right:** Dr Whitcombe made a pilgrimage to Portstewart in Northern Ireland in 1925 to see the steam locomotives of the Portstewart tramway. He found them 'as good as new', drove No 3 several times, and was astonished at the silent and smooth running. The line closed in 1926. Through Dr Whitcombe's efforts, locomotive No 1 was transferred to Hull Transport Museum in 1939; No 2 is now in Belfast Transport Museum. This view gives a good idea of the scenic nature of the tramway which was opened in 1882 to connect the railway station with the resort of Portstewart. **Right:** A late survivor among English steam tramways was the Wantage Tramway; passenger service continued until 1925 and goods traffic until 1945. Here Matthews locomotive No 6 of about 1880 and car No 4 prepare to depart from Wantage Road station for the town of Wantage in 1912. The car was built in 1900 by Hurst Nelson as an electric double-decker and was later converted.

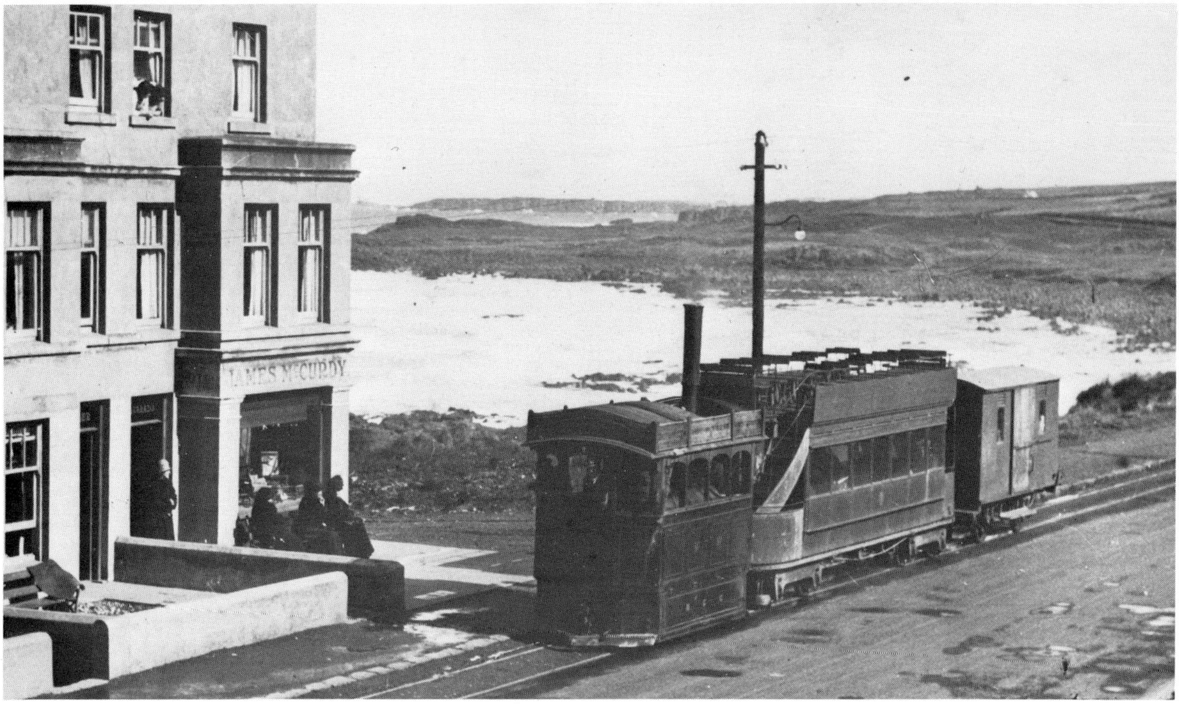
JAMES McCURDY

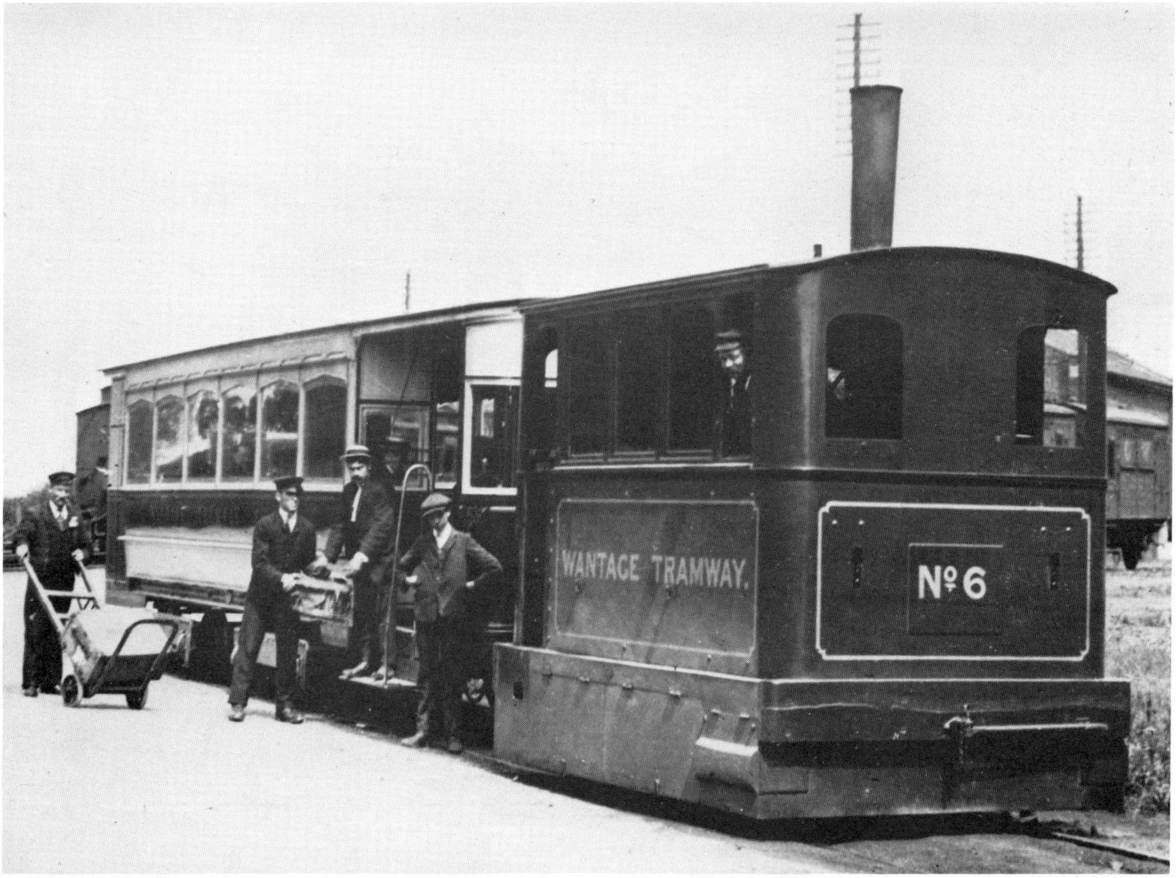
WANTAGE TRAMWAY.
No 6

Cable Cars

Cable trams showed their merits particularly well in hilly towns; hence two of their most renowned strongholds were Edinburgh **(left)**, which had the most extensive system in Britain, and San Francisco **(right)** where this method of operation originated in 1873. Edinburgh's first cable cars started in 1888 and the last did not cease until 1922, while some cable cars in San Francisco are still running. San Francisco initially favoured the separate grip car ('dummy') hauling a passenger trailer, while Edinburgh used single vehicles, including the open and covered-top double-deckers shown. The 'gripper', which passed beneath the track to transmit the motion of the cable to the car, can just be discerned under the car in this view.

The short cable tramway on Constitution Hill in Swansea **(above)** had a brief life, lasting only from 1898 to 1903. The two cars passed on a loop midway along the line, and an overhead wire was used for signalling purposes. A cable car in Edinburgh **(left)**, which at one time had a fleet of over 200 such vehicles; the 'capstan' for controlling the gripper can be seen on the platform. Note also the substantial track brake blocks between the bogie wheels; special braking devices were needed for the steep gradients.

Right: What made the cables go: this interior view of Hockley cable house in Birmingham reveals the machinery that was needed to keep the cables moving. The longest cable was over six miles long. **Below:** Men, and women, of the footplate in Birmingham and Edinburgh respectively. Driving a cable car required skill and judgement, especially where junctions necessitated the dropping and picking up of the cable with split-second accuracy if an inextricable tangle was to be avoided!

Oil and Gas

Left: Early experiments in mechanical traction for tramways included the oil-engined *Connelly Motor* which underwent trials in London at Greenwich and Croydon in 1893. It pulled an ordinary car carrying 40 passengers and was described as 'maintaining the Board of Trade regulation speed of eight miles an hour easily, and being evidently capable of a far higher speed'. Nevertheless horse haulage was soon resumed.
Below: Gas was another source of power. Early gas-driven cars were said to run 'quietly and easily, emitting neither smoke nor steam, and quite under control', though a contemporary observer wrote that 'the cars vibrate in an unpleasant manner, and the less said about the smell the better'. In South Wales, Neath operated gas-engined cars of the type shown here on their route from Skewen to Briton Ferry from 1903 to 1920. The doors of the engine compartment can be seen in the side of the car; the semi-circular plate covered part of the large flywheel of the engine.

Above: Petrol and diesel-engined cars were employed on several tramways where the traffic did not warrant the expense of fixed electrical equipment. This is an example in Rotterdam in the 1920s on the Overschie route, on which steam and horse power also had their day. **Below:** Another early gas-engined car, belonging to the Traction Syndicate of London and Dresden and constructed to Lührig's design. **Right:** Among the earliest petrol-engined cars to be used on a street tramway, this vehicle was put into service at Morecambe in 1912. The driver sat beside his engine in approved motor bus fashion. Morecambe owned a small fleet of such vehicles until the route was taken over by buses in 1924.

Above: In Holland, the Gooische tramways ran petrol and diesel cars on their former steam routes which extended from Amsterdam to Hilversum and Laren. Notice the locomotive-style coupling rods on the right-hand bogie of this car. **Centre left:** A Simplex petrol-engined car in Karachi. The Karachi tramways introduced such vehicles in 1910 and successfully operated a fleet of about 60 on their busy town routes for many years, latterly with diesel engines; the last of them were not withdrawn until 1975. **Bottom left:** This Drewry petrol-engined car was supplied in 1926 for the Dublin and Blessington tramway, where it took its place among the steam trams on this roadside line. Note the unusual wheel arrangement. The car was later converted from 5ft 3in gauge to 3ft for the County Donegal Railways.

Electric Trams

While many methods of electric operation were tried, the overhead wire was proved to be generally the most practicable. Berlin car No 1 of the 1890s **(above)** carries the name of one of the pioneer firms of electric traction, Siemens and Halske. More than 40 cities and towns in Germany had electric tramways by 1896, and over 110 by 1901. In Britain, the first street tramway to use the overhead wire and trolley pole was inaugurated in Leeds in 1891. The initial fleet of single-deckers soon gave way to the typically British open-top double-deckers **(right)**. The smart turnout of No 85 and its crew reflects civic pride in the new mode of transport. By 1900 Britain had 1,000 miles of tramways.

Above: The time of transition. In Paris, new tracks being laid for electric cars; because overhead wires were considered unsightly, the conduit system was installed, employing conductor rails beneath the track and a central slot for the 'plough' to convey current to the car. Note the outer tracks in the street still being used by steam trams. **Centre left:** With the conduit costing 30-50 per cent more to construct, most undertakings favoured the overhead wire. To install and maintain the overhead equipment, the tower wagon was an essential member of the fleet. Ready for action is this horse-drawn example in Birmingham. **Bottom left:** New and old: a historic moment in Rochdale as an electric car poses with the steam tram it is superseding. Note that the electric car reverts to the open top deck now that there is no longer any smoke or soot to besmirch the 'outside' passenger. By the early years of this century most of the urban steamers had gone.

DUBLIN
DUBLIN ELECTRIC TRAMWAYS
DUBLIN ELECTRIC TRAMWAYS

SPECIAL CAR
SPECIAL CAR
LEDGER
DERBY CORPORATION

The introduction of the new electric cars was generally heralded with due ceremony. **Left:** The opening of the Dublin to Dalkey line in 1896, with the great tramway entrepreneur Clifton Robinson at the controls. The car is by Milnes and hauls a trailer; note the prominent oil headlamp. **Bottom left:** Wet weather probably did not dampen the enthusiasm as Derby Corporation started their electric trams in 1904. **Above right:** To the delight of posterity (and local youngsters!) the new trams were duly recorded by enthusiastic photographers; this is Belfast in 1905. **Centre right:** Almost a surrealistic impression of the electric tramway era: nearly the whole fleet of the Cork undertaking can be seen in this view taken during a suspension of service. **Below:** The new electric car offered greater speed and comfort than its contemporary the horse bus: the two forms of transport in Hastings about 1906.

To enable the upper deck to earn useful revenue in all weathers, many of the original open toppers soon had covers fitted; here are the first top covers in Halifax **(left)** and Sheffield **(below)** in 1903. The Halifax example could be opened up in fine weather. On the opposite page by contrast are Paris fashions in double-deckers. While some Continental systems introduced double-deckers in early days, the single-decker eventually enjoyed almost a monopoly.

INCENNES-EXPOSITION
CHEMINS DE FER NOGENTAIS
TRACTION ELECTRIQUE
Nº 4
Nº 7

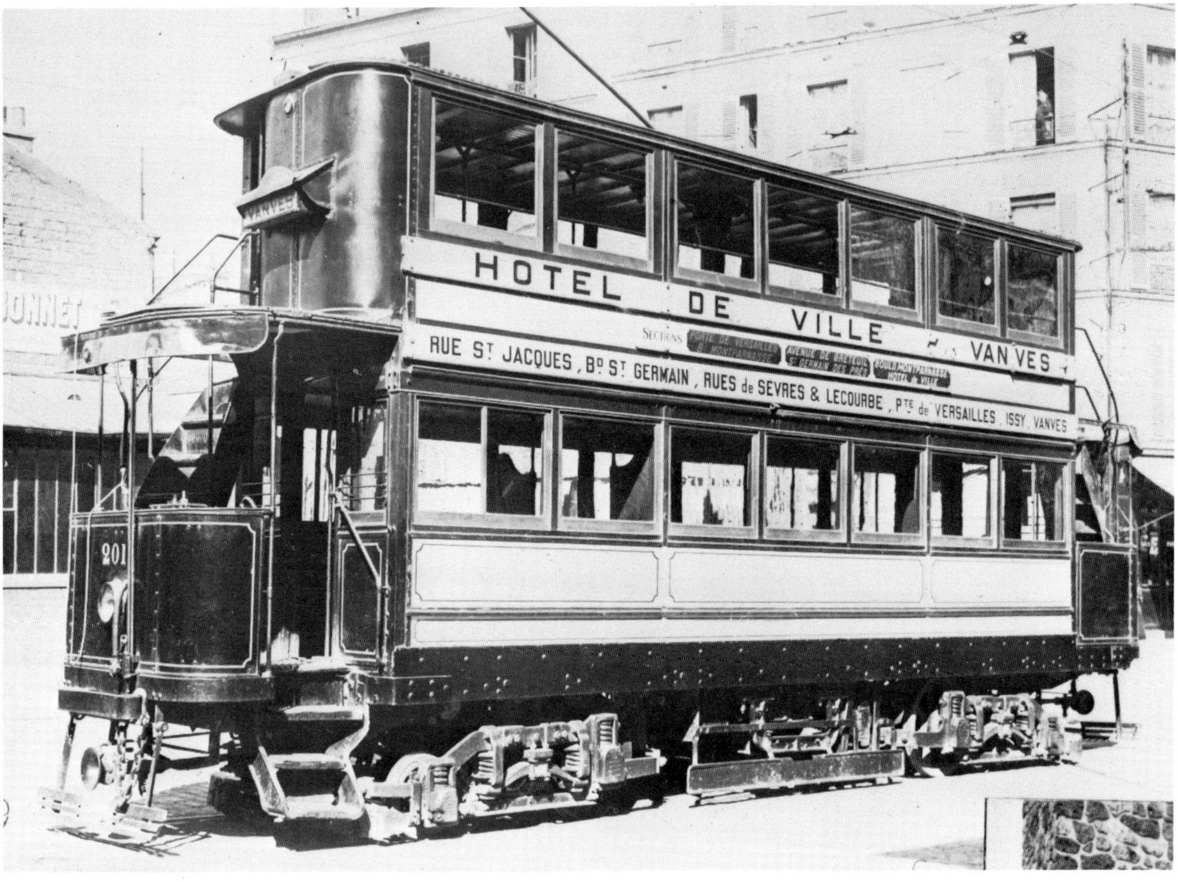
VANVES
HOTEL DE VILLE VANVES
SECTIONS
RUE St JACQUES, Bd St GERMAIN, RUES de SEVRES & LECOURBE, Pte de VERSAILLES, ISSY, VANVES
201

A study in single-deckers. **Above:** Blackburn Corporation No 76, a 1905-vintage closed combination car by Milnes mounted on Brill 22E trucks, decorated for the Coronation of King George V in 1911. British urban tramways generally turned to single-deckers only when such features as low bridges made it impracticable to run double-deckers. **Centre right:** The open-sided cross-bench car had a high seating capacity and was popular in parts of the world where the climate favoured travel in such exposed vehicles. This one served in Kingston, Jamaica. **Bottom right:** More suited to the cold northern climes was the all-enclosed car, complete with platform doors; this example from the Stockholm fleet of the 1920s is fairly typical of Continental European practice. It is fitted with a pantograph current collector.

Trams of Empire

Cape to Cairo: even if the dream of a Cape to Cairo railway never materialised, at least there were trams at both extremities. British influence (and British capital) brought the big double-decker, such as this one **(above)** in Cape Town, where the first electric cars started in 1896. Cairo **(left)** also had electric trams in 1896, installed by a Belgian company; a large fleet of more modern cars is still in operation.

Farther east to Imperial India, where the single decker again held sway. **Above:** A uni-directional motor and trailer in Calcutta, where horse trams started in 1881 and the first electric line was put into regular service in 1902. Trams are still hard at work in Calcutta today. **Centre right:** Madras had horse trams as early as 1874, and after a British-owned company was established in 1892 the first electric tramway started in 1895, initially using the conduit system. Trams continued to run until 1953. **Bottom right:** An interesting design in Rangoon in 1905; note the small enclosed saloon at one end.

Left: In Australia, Sydney's first electric tramway was a short experimental line opened in 1890 with American cars and equipment. It lasted until 1892 before reverting to steam traction. Electric cars soon reappeared, however, to grow into a fleet of over 1,700, the largest in Australia. The crew here have the appearance of traditional Colonial characters of the period! **Below:** To Christchurch in New Zealand, where an electric car can just be seen coming in by the side entrance to the depot. Electrification took place in 1905, but steamer No 9 was still serviceable when this photograph was taken in 1920.

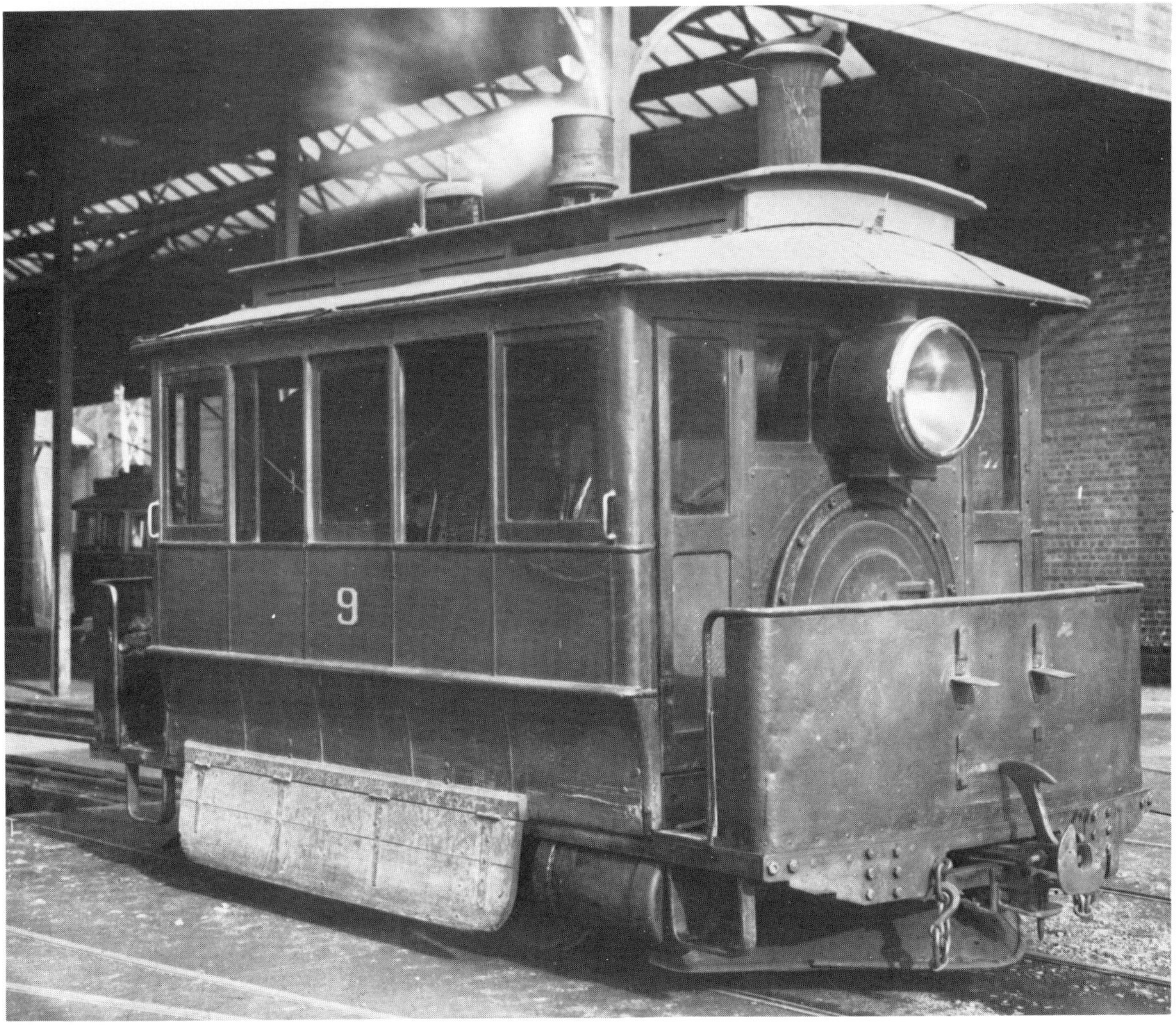

A study in size: almost the two extremes in double-deck dimension. **Above:** A four wheeler of the Cork system on the unusually narrow gauge of 2ft 11½in. **Below:** A massive bogie car of the Cape Town Tramways. The large passenger capacity of the big tram gave it an advantage over the smaller bus and helped to prolong its life on many busy city routes.

Interlude ~ Curious Cars

Most trams were designed to carry passengers, but here are two that were not: **(below)** the Tramway and Motor Express which provided a parcels service on the Birmingham and Midland Tramways; and **(bottom)** a horse-drawn goods tram at Groningen in Holland.

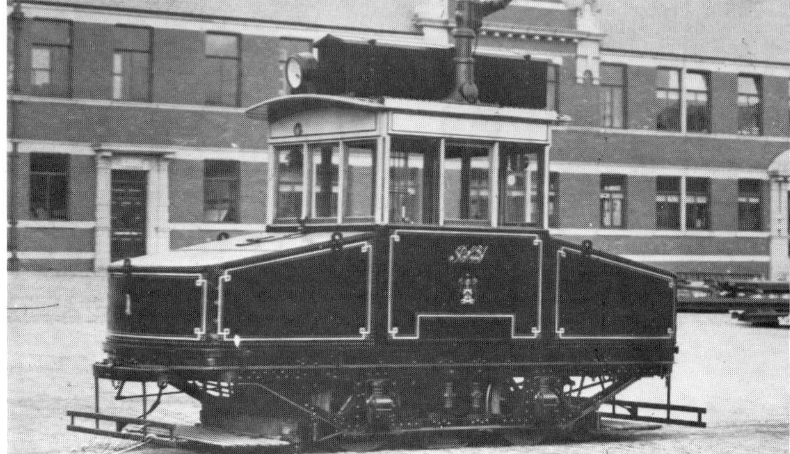

Above: This rather fearsome looking machine is a Krauss double-deck steam car built for Munich in 1882. The design almost anticipates the steam rail-motors introduced on several British railways in the early years of the twentieth century. **Centre right:** A neat steeple-cab electric locomotive employed on the tramways of Burnley. **Bottom right:** The 'Golfer's Tram'; the London and North Eastern Railway ran a tramway to give access from the station to its hotel at Cruden Bay in Scotland. One of the few electric tramways owned by a British main-line railway company, it continued to convey hotel patrons until 1932.

PART 2

Through Dr Whitcombe's Camera

In 1927 over 14,000 trams were at work in the British Isles; this proved to be the zenith, for after that year an accelerating decline reduced the total to some 8,000 by 1939. Photographs taken during the late 1920s are therefore of exceptional interest in depicting scenes that were very soon to vanish, and such is the case with this selection of Dr Whitcombe's photographs which comprise the second half of this volume. Here are trams, some dating from the earliest days of electric operation, seen almost literally in their last days, and often bearing the scars of a long hard life. In the above view of Rochdale, for example, one of the 1912 single deckers on the route to Bamford stands at its town centre terminus in industrial Lancashire; all Rochdale's trams were withdrawn between 1930 and 1932.

The work of a dedicated amateur, Dr Whitcombe's photographs possess an engaging air of informality quite unlike the official pictures. The trams are caught in their everyday settings, busy at their daily tasks rather than in their Sunday best. And notice how many of the photographs happen to include people; not only does this human interest add vitality to the scenes, but it serves to recall the part played by the trams in the town dweller's life for so many years.

The review concludes with a glance overseas, a reminder that in numerous cities in Continental Europe the tram continues to flourish, albeit in a form very different from that of half a century ago.

London and South

Britain's greatest tramway system, London in the late-1920s had some 2,700 trams owned by both companies and municipalities. Western suburbs were served by the London United Tramways, two of whose cars are seen on this page. **Right:** No 332, one of 40 T class built by the United Electric Car Company in 1906 and later reconditioned, carries the short-lived paint style of this period. **Below:** No 286, one of the Milnes-built U class dating from 1902 and originally with open top deck. Both vehicles are at the Shepherds Bush terminus. Note the peculiar angular stairway favoured by the LUT. Extensive replacement by trolleybuses was undertaken during the 1930s.

Above: At the heart of the London network were the lines of the London County Council, owners of more than 1,700 cars. Most were bogie double-deckers, but here is one of the four-wheel C class dating from 1904. It is travelling along the Victoria Embankment, used as a terminal loop by numerous routes. Lines in the inner areas were worked on the conduit system, since overhead wires were not permitted, and some cars were not fitted with trolley poles. **Centre left:** LCC cars terminated at suburban Abbey Wood, and just around the corner were the tracks of Erith Urban District Council. Here Erith No 3, a Brush-built open topper of 1906, prepares to leave for Bexleyheath. **Bottom left:** Nearby Bexley Council's No 14 travels through Plumstead on its way to Horns Cross, furthest southeast terminus of the London lines. No 14 was built in 1904 by the Electric Railway and Tramway Carriage Works and was one of many older trams withdrawn after the London Passenger Transport Board was formed in 1933.

Right: Hastings Tramways No 45 traverses the private right of way across Pebsham Marsh on the route between Hastings and Bexhill. This seaside system started in 1905 and at various times used surface-contact electrification and petrol-electric cars. Trolleybuses took over in 1929. **Below:** Maidstone Corporation No 11, a 1907 UEC car on a Brill truck, was working the short Tovil route when photographed here. The route was replaced by buses in 1929.

To the Midlands

Left: No 11 of Luton Corporation was a UEC car introduced for the start of tramway operation in the town in 1908. As with many smaller systems it remained virtually unchanged until abandonment, in this case in 1932.
Below: Another of the smaller systems, Northampton had a variety of rolling stock including this lengthy bogie single-decker, as well as open toppers of the kind visible in the background.

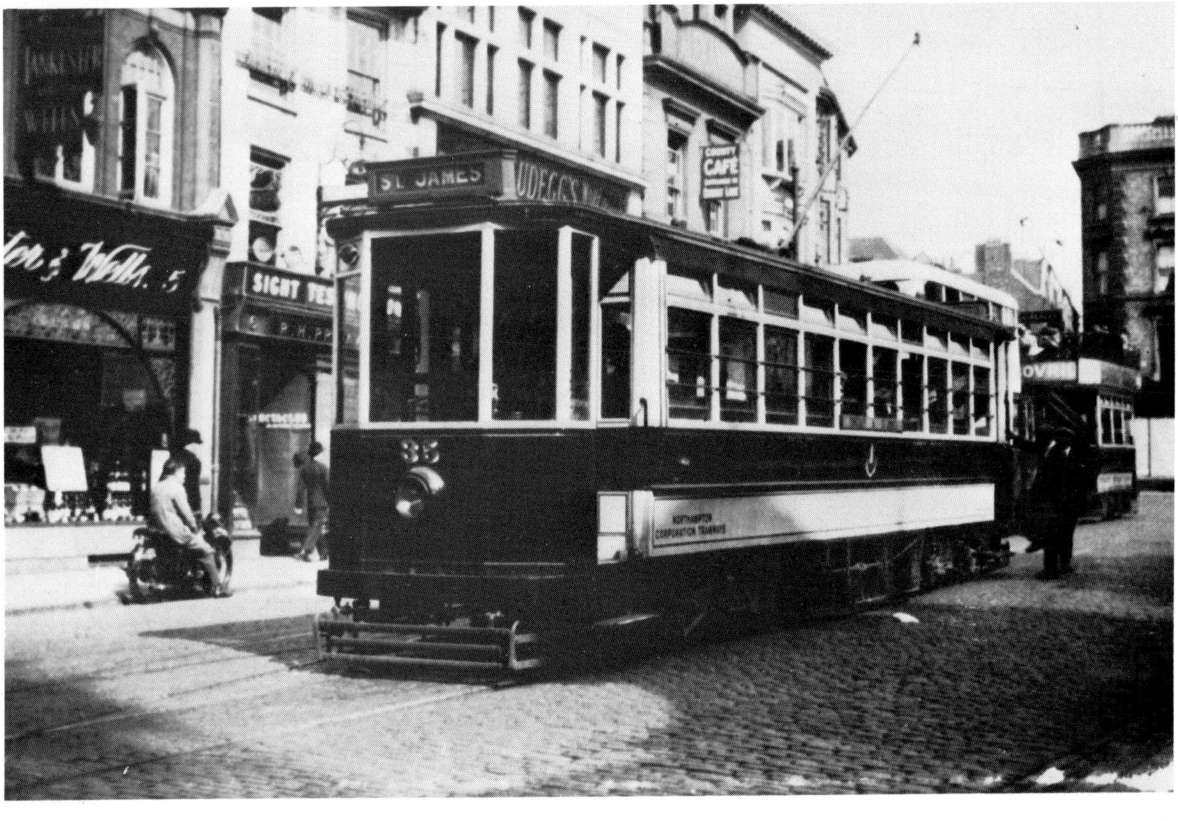

Above: A real veteran even at this time, Coventry No 13 was one of eight cars supplied in 1897-8 with a Falcon-built body on Peckham cantilever truck. It was still in peak-hour service up to 1932. The route symbol can just be observed above the advertisement board. **Right:** A busy scene on the 3ft 6in gauge Black Country tramways at Bilston Town Hall, with South Staffs double decker No 41 bound for Wednesbury and a Wolverhampton District single-decker on the route to Fighting Cocks. No 41 is a Brush-built car of 1904-5, while the single-decker is a standard car of the Birmingham and Midland Tramways Joint Committee following the success of the 1917 prototype. The angular vestibule protrusions on the double-decker allowed room for the controls.

Trams have generally made little mark in literature, but there are exceptions. **Above:** The Potteries trams are immortalised in Arnold Bennett's stories of the Five Towns. Here is one in real life; dating from 1900, it was in its last days when photographed here; the Potteries trams were replaced by buses in 1928. **Left:** The Nottinghamshire and Derbyshire company's trams feature in the works of D. H. Lawrence whose native country was the company's Nottingham to Ripley route through Eastwood. No 17 was scrapped in 1931; observe its condition, and the figures that could almost be characters from a Lawrence story!

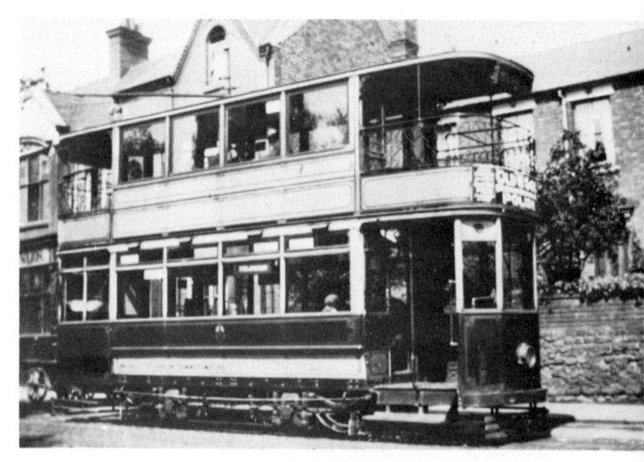

Top right: On another part of the Black Country network, Walsall employed open-balcony double-deckers of this type dating from 1912 and 1919 until operations ceased in 1933. Early routes built by the South Staffordshire Tramways had been acquired by the Corporation, which also constructed further routes. **Centre right:** The small system of Ilkeston Corporation, opened in 1903, was taken over by the Nottinghamshire and Derbyshire company in 1917, although the two systems were not physically connected. Here Ilkeston No 8, one of the eight survivors, makes an apparently lightly loaded journey not long before its demise at the beginning of 1931. **Below:** Dr Whitcombe was only just in time to photograph the Matlock cable tramway which ceased operation in 1927. Opened in 1893, the half-mile 3ft 6in gauge line had a maximum gradient of 1 in 5½ and had three of these Milnes-built cars.

West and Wales

Above: The oddly-shaped platform screen was one of the few improvements made over the years to this open-top Brush double-decker in Gloucester where the last tramways survived until 1933. **Below:** A 1904 vintage Milnes-built open topper of Bath Electric Tramways, typical of a relatively extensive system which served this historic city up to 1939. **Right:** Again a characteristic open topper, this car worked on the Newport tramways, some routes of which ran until 1937.

In the Welsh Valleys. **Right:** Obviously a fine day in Aberdare when No 24 was caught with a good load of passengers on its open top deck as it makes its way to Trecynon. Aberdare's trams continued to operate until 1935. **Below:** Not so fine in Merthyr, to judge by the screens protecting the driver — and surely obscuring his view! This car of the Merthyr Tydfil Traction and Lighting Company is on the route to Dowlais which functioned until 1937.

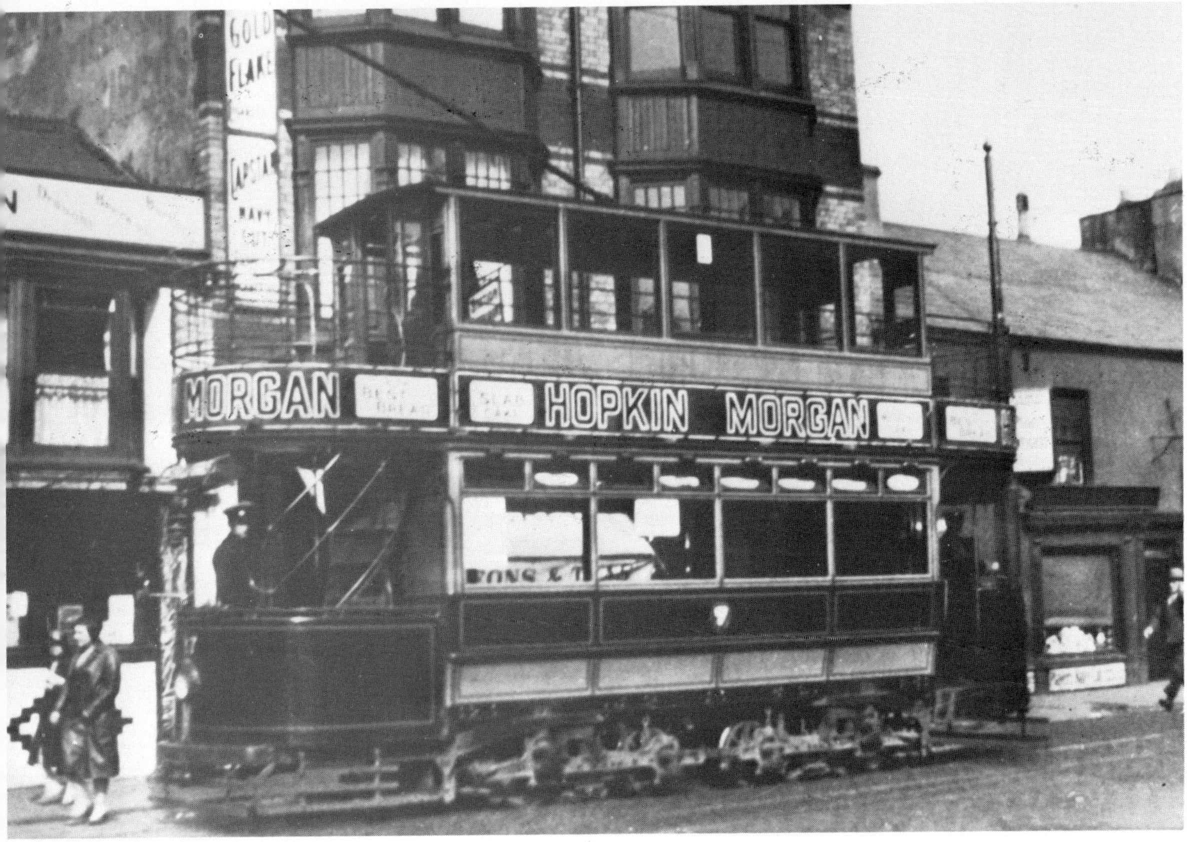

Two top-covered bogie cars of Pontypridd Urban District Council, whose lines connected with those of the Rhondda Tramways Company to permit through services to Porth. Pontypridd withdrew its trams in 1931.

BLACK & WHITE WHISKY
PORTH
GUMMER'S THE QUALITY GROCERS. PORTH.

Puritan Soap
Puritan Soap

Above left: Cars of the Rhondda Tramways Company in the Porth depot. The background scenery gives an idea of the terrain through which the fleet of some 50 trams operated to reach Maerdy and Treherbert. **Left:** Further west to the depot of the Llanelly and District Electric Supply Company, whose trams operated until replaced by trolleybuses in 1933. **Above:** To North Wales, where among the early rolling stock of the Llandudno and Colwyn Bay Electric Railway was No 16, a 'semi-convertible' single-decker constructed by UEC in 1909. In later years this popular seaside line was served by large bogie cars. **Right:** Back into England, to the small Chester system where this 1903 Milnes-built open topper ran until 1930.

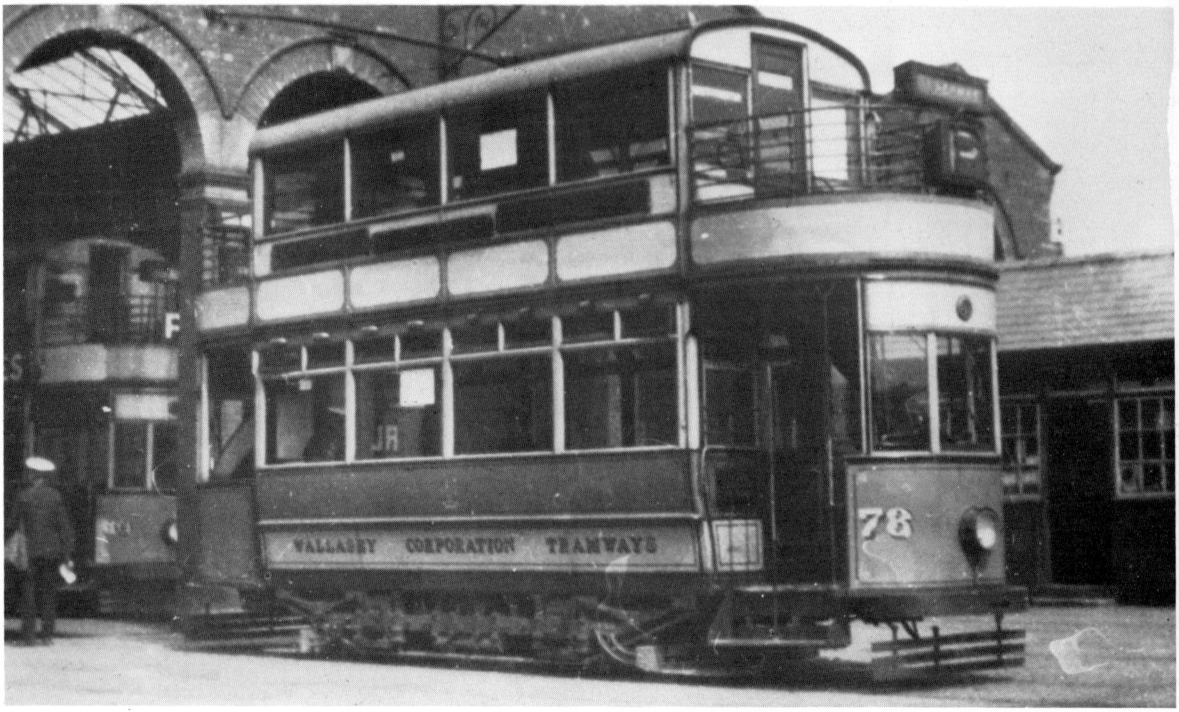

North West

Dating from 1920, No 78 **(above)** was the last new car supplied to the Wallasey tramways. It is a Brush-built vehicle on a Peckham P22 truck. The South Lancashire Tramways **(left)**, headquartered at Atherton, operated services to Leigh, Ashton-in-Makerfield and Farnworth, connecting with the municipal lines of St Helens, Wigan, Bolton and Salford. Cars of Wigan **(above right)** and St Helens **(right)**, both parts of the great network of tracks that extended across industrial south Lancashire. The St Helens double-decker is on a shortlived through service to Wigan in 1927-8; this used a specially laid connection at Ashton-in-Makerfield, where No 6 is seen.

DEPOT
WIGAN CORPORATION TRAMWAYS

McDOUG
WIGAN
ST HELENS CORPORATION TRAMWAYS

CORPORATION TRAMWAYS

PENWORTHAM
YCLISTS REST
CYCLISTS REST

More Lancashire tramcars. **Above left:** One of Warrington's original Milnes cars of 1902 after being rebuilt with a top cover during the fleet reconstruction of the 1920s. **Left:** A Preston Corporation UEC car of 1904 vintage; again it originally had an open top deck. **Above:** A scene in Ashton with Corporation cars of single and double-deck types. **Right:** One of Salford's original 1901-2 fleet of Milnes open toppers. Formerly No 5, this car had recently been renumbered when this photograph was taken at Whitefield on the Bury Old Road route. Note the side destination boards and the elaborate lining-out still applied.

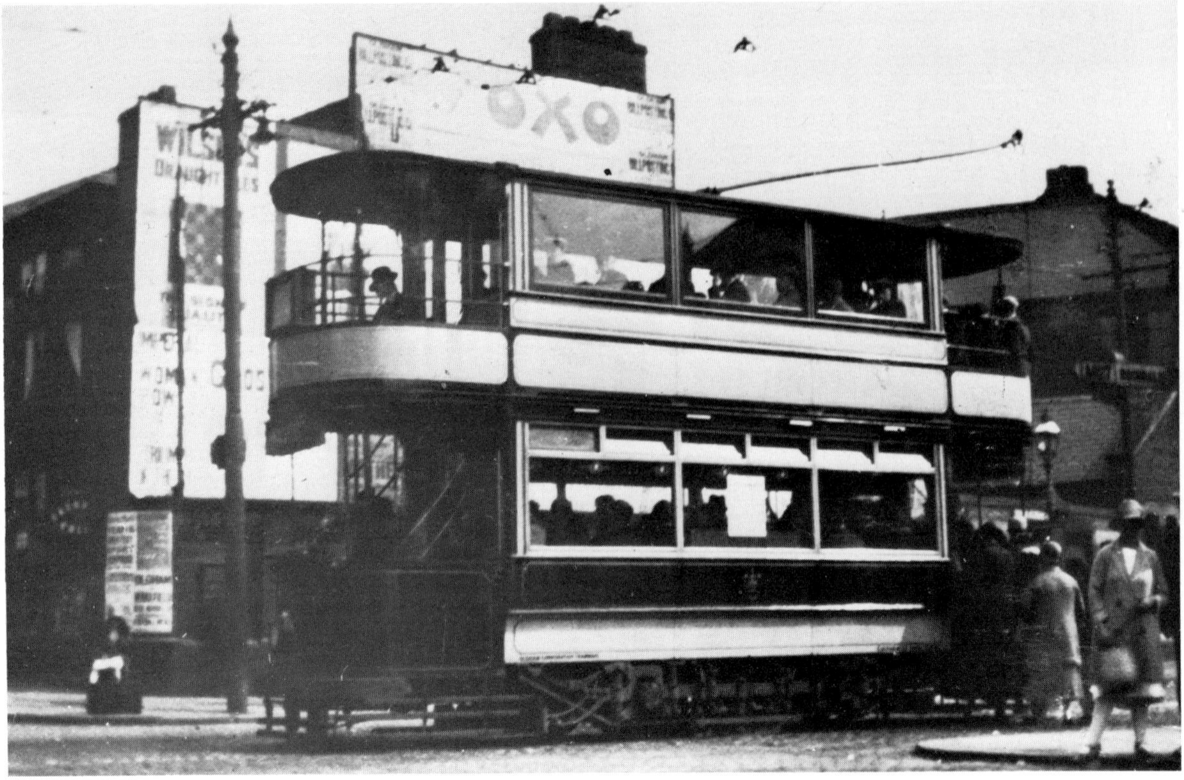
OXO

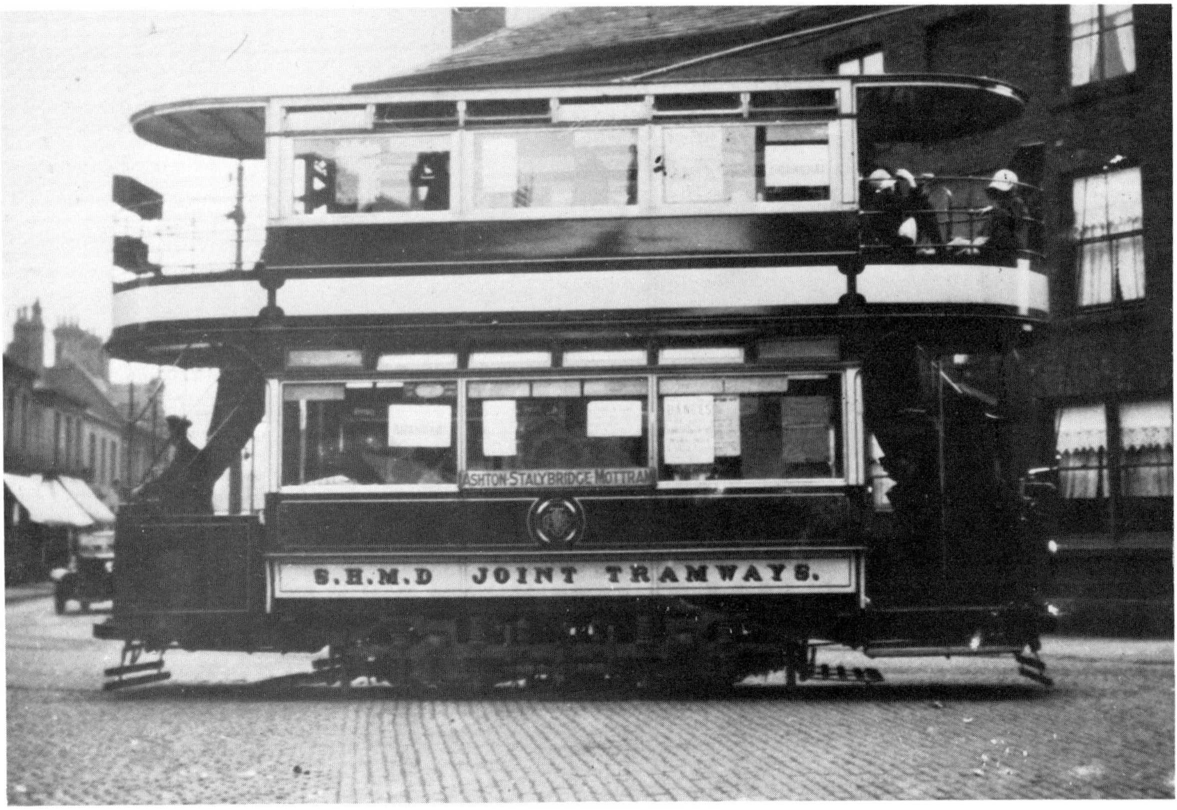
ASHTON-STALYBRIDGE-MOTTRAM
S.H.M.D JOINT TRAMWAYS.

Left: When this photograph was taken in 1927, Oldham Corporation owned a fleet of some 120 trams, mostly open-balcony double-deckers like this one. **Below left:** A typical balcony car of the Stalybridge, Hyde, Mossley and Dukinfield Joint Board in action on the Ashton-Mottram route. **Right:** Blackburn's water car No 1 glimpsed on one of its rare outings handling a load of rails. **Below:** Bolton's Brush-built No 138 was one of eight bought in 1924 from the Sunderland District company, for which they had been constructed in 1920.

Left: Accrington No 26, a Brush car of 1912 on a Brush truck, is seen on the through service to Rawtenstall. **Below:** Burnley's single-deck No 45 of 1903 was of UEC origin and mounted on Brill 27G maximum-traction trucks. **Above right:** An animated scene in Carlisle as open-top No 4 prepares to leave for Newton (note the stop sign on the central standard). **Below right:** A contrasting view with this long bogie single-decker of Barrow-in-Furness.

NEWTOWN
WEAR
DURAFIT
SUITS
CO-OPERATIVE STORES
BOTCHERGATE
SAWYER, CHEMIST

BARROW IN FURNESS CORPORATION TRAMWAYS 20

East and North

Right: Norwich No 27, one of the original 1900-vintage cars on the largest undertaking in East Anglia; it has a Brush body with seats for 26 inside and 26 out. **Below:** The Peterborough Electric Traction Company started operations in 1902-3 with 12 Brush cars like this one; services ceased in 1930.

Left: Sheffield had its first electric trams in 1899, and by the late 1920s had over 400 cars on 50 miles of routes. **Below:** Mexborough and Swinton No 11, one of the company's original Dick Kerr open toppers of 1902, was fitted with a lowheight top cover with offset trolley pole to get under a low bridge; it is seen here only just before abandonment in 1929.

Above: An English Electric single-decker running on one of the last-built and shortest-lived tramways, the Dearne District Light Railway which opened in 1924 and closed in 1933.

Right: Barnsley's own trams ended in 1930, and this Brush car of Barnsley and District looks as though it has seen better days. **Below:** The Yorkshire Woollen District Tramways worked a 22-mile network of lines around the Dewsbury area, serving the towns of Batley, Heckmondwike and Cleckheaton. The company's No 80 was one of 12 single-deckers brought from Sheffield in 1919-20. **Bottom:** Most of the Woollen District fleet consisted of double-deckers such as No 34, a Brush car of 1903 and originally an open topper. Note the distinctive high ends to the balcony, and the reversed stairs. The hand bell, used instead of a foot gong, is just visible hanging under the stairs.

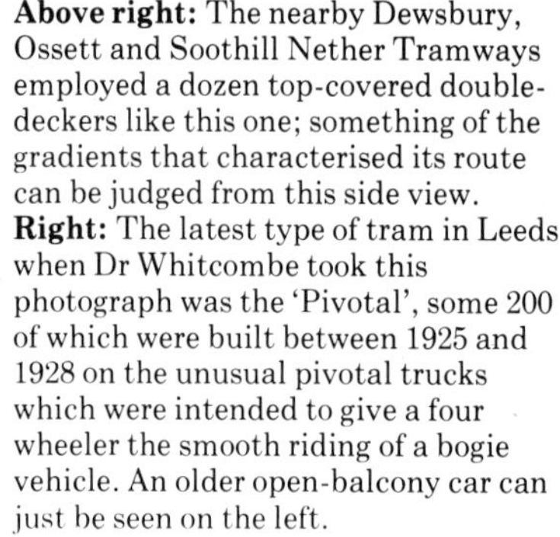

Above right: The nearby Dewsbury, Ossett and Soothill Nether Tramways employed a dozen top-covered double-deckers like this one; something of the gradients that characterised its route can be judged from this side view. **Right:** The latest type of tram in Leeds when Dr Whitcombe took this photograph was the 'Pivotal', some 200 of which were built between 1925 and 1928 on the unusual pivotal trucks which were intended to give a four wheeler the smooth riding of a bogie vehicle. An older open-balcony car can just be seen on the left.

BICKERS
FOR LINENS
Players
Navy Cut
DEWSBURY & OSSETT TRAMWAYS

10
MELBOURNE ALES

A contrast in Bradford. **Left:** A balcony double-decker of the type built by the Corporation between 1912 and 1931 for its 4ft gauge system. Bradford had some 250 trams serving nearly 60 miles of routes. **Below:** Almost brand-new when this photograph was taken, Bradford's No 1 was put into service in 1927. Designed and built by the Transport Department as an experiment, it remained the only one of its kind. With bodywork in varnished mahogany, No 1 had outside coupling rods on the bogie wheels, and was said to have attained a speed of over 50mph. **Right:** Huddersfield's No 53 was built in 1902 by UEC with an open top deck but was later given this short cover. **Below right:** Still a fairly new car at this time, Halifax No 105 was one of three single-deckers built by the Corporation in 1924. Note the front exit and short clerestory; also the 'five-bar gate' effect of the long-wheelbase truck.

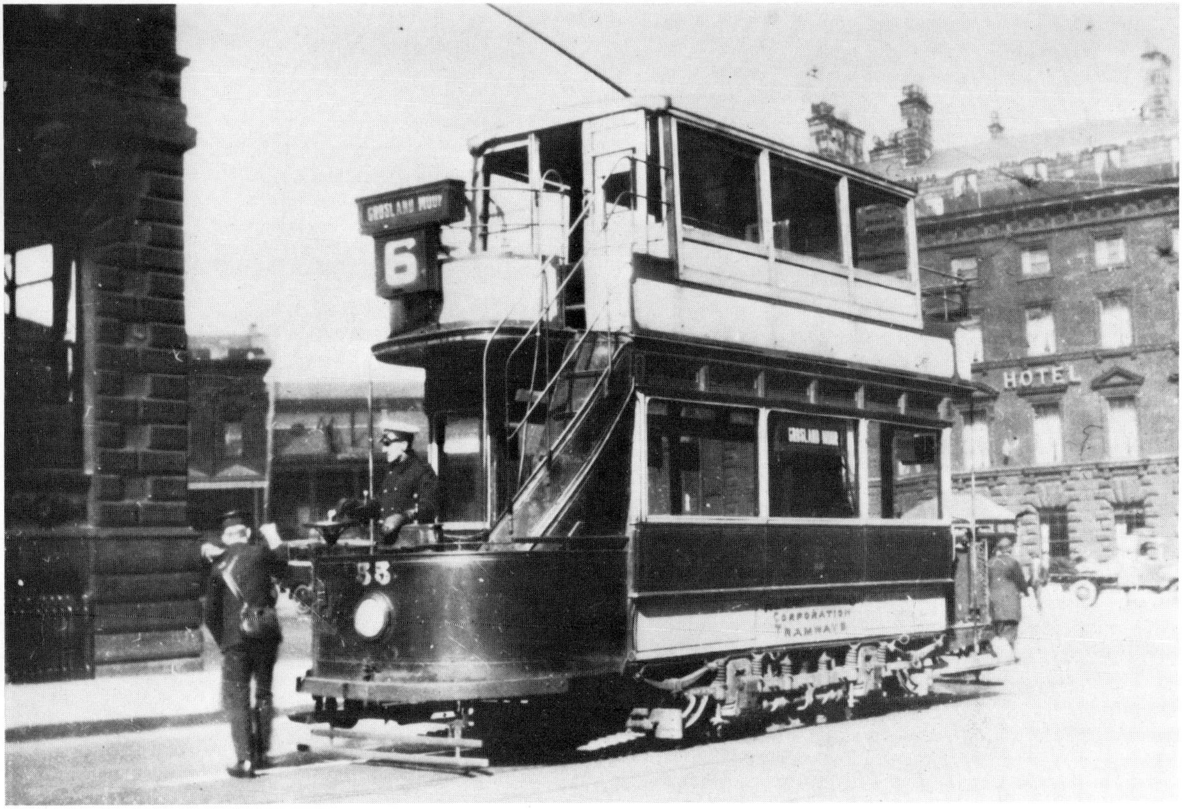
6
HOTEL
CORPORATION
TRAMWAYS

8
HALIFAX CORPORATION TRAMWAYS

NORTON
HEINZ SPAGHETTI
127
MIDDLESBROUGH CORPORATION TRAMWAYS

HEINZ TOMATO KETCHUP 57
106
SPRING CLEANING
CARPETS
LINOS
LOOSE COVERS
NEWHOUSE'S
MIDDLESBROUGH CORPORATION TRAMWAYS

On Teesside, two of the Imperial Tramways Company's cars taken over by Middlesbrough Corporation in 1921. **Above left:** No 127, one of 50 built by Milnes on Peckham reversed maximum-traction bogies. **Left:** No 106, one of 10 single-deck combination cars, again by Milnes on Maguire maximum-traction trucks. **Above:** Trams of two operators at Cleethorpes: a car of Great Grimsby Street Tramways on the right works a Cleethorpes route, while the Grimsby Corporation car on the left is on the Grimsby route which the Corporation took over in 1925. **Right:** A car on the 3ft 6in gauge York tramways.

Jarrow and District No 9 **(left)** the Brush 'show car' of 1902 but later rebuilt, was still at work shortly before the abandonment of the town's tramways in 1929. In Sunderland, a 1901 single-decker **(below)** by Dick Kerr as later rebuilt and used on the Villette Road route until 1930. In contrast, nearby Newcastle seemed to go in for really big trams **(above right)** known as the 'submarines' from the conning-tower appearance of their short open top deck, the C class had started life in 1902 as single-deckers built by Hurst Nelson. The 'Front Exit Car' sign indicates the passenger-flow method widely used in Newcastle. Even more massive was this F class double decker **(below right)** built by the Corporation in 1903 with a seating capacity of 84.

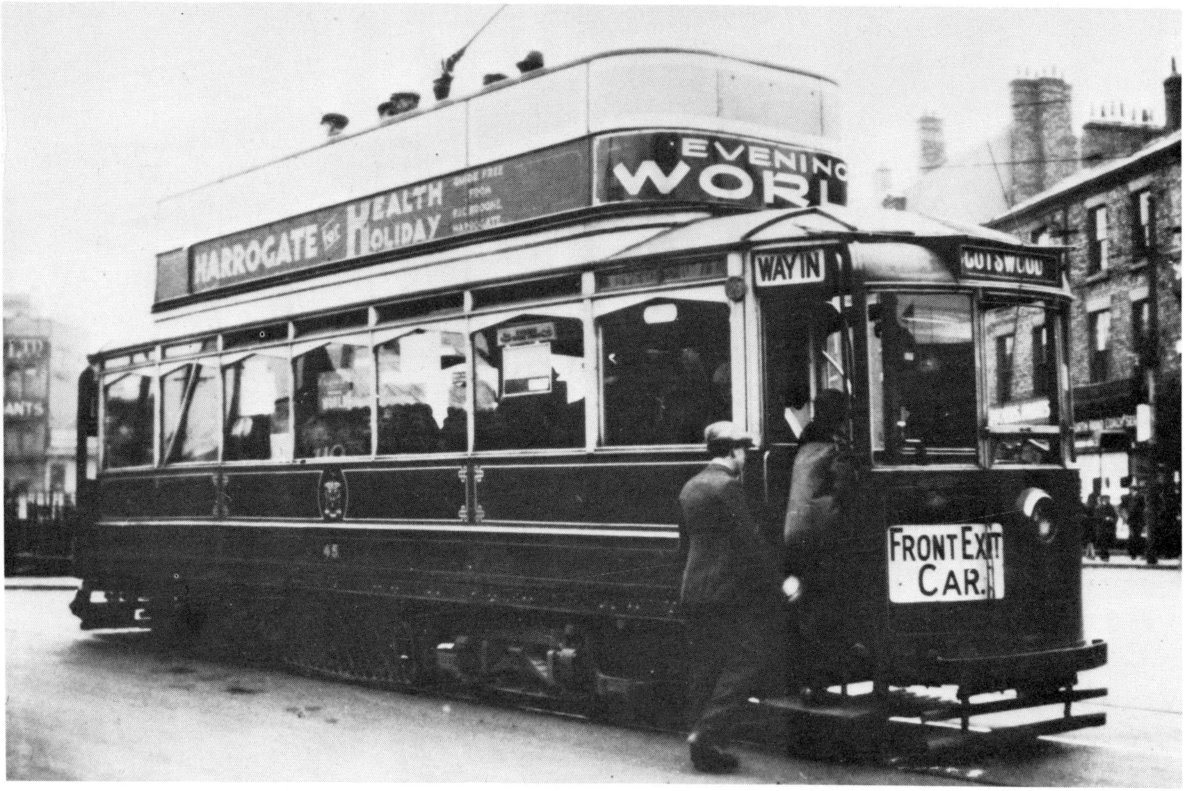
EVENING
WORL
HARROGATE for HEALTH HOLIDAY
WAY IN
COTSWOOD
FRONT EXIT CAR.

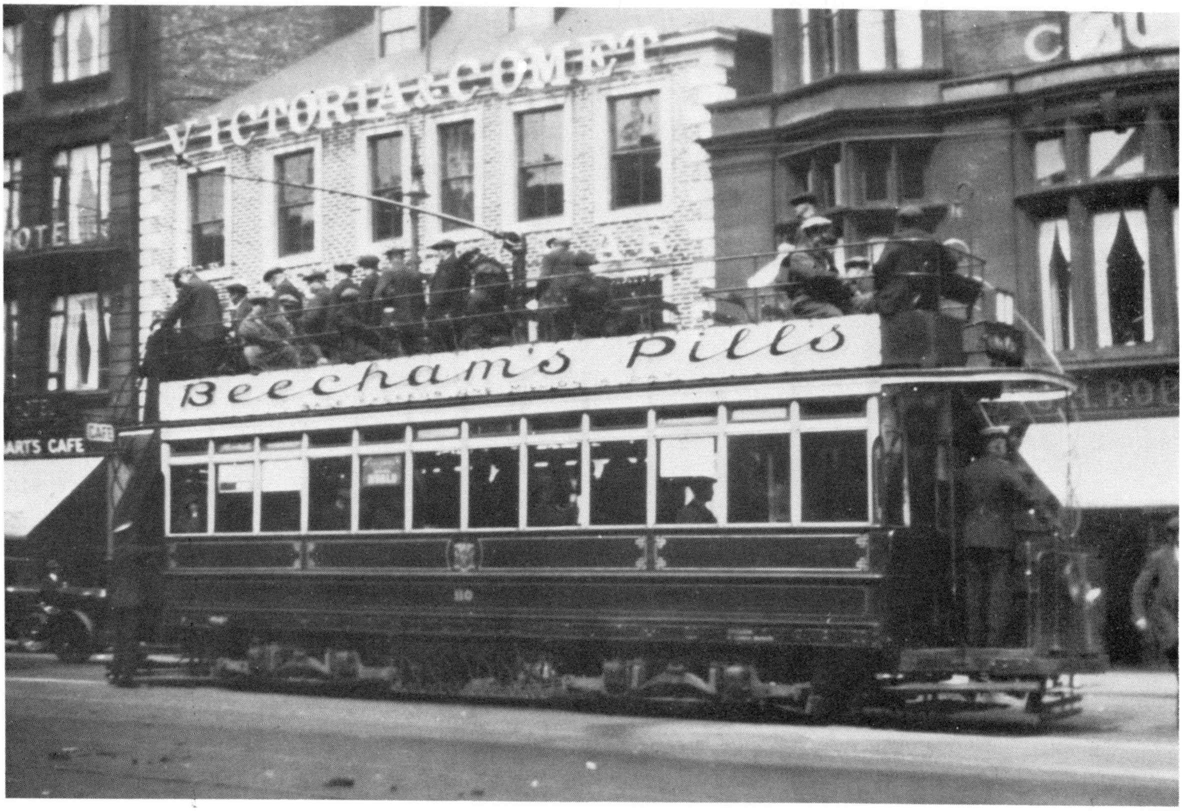
VICTORIA & COMET
HOTE
Beecham's Pills
ARTS CAFE
CAFE

The Tyneside Tramways and Tramroads Company ran between Gosforth and North Shields on the periphery of Newcastle, much of the route being on private right of way **(right)**, while **(below)** the Tynemouth and District Tramways ran from North Shields to Whitley Bay. Tyneside No 8 is a 1902 Milnes car on a Brill 21E truck, while the Tynemouth car has a body acquired second-hand from the Burton and Ashby tramway and mounted on an old Brill truck. The Tyneside system ceased in 1930, and Tynemouth the following year.

Scotland

Above/Left: Probably the most scenic tram route in Scotland was the Rothesay Tramways' five miles on the Isle of Bute from Rothesay to Ettrick Bay. The 3ft 6in gauge cars were single-deckers of both the open toastrack type and the roofed combination design. **Bottom left:** The tramways of Ayr had their historic appeal, with a main route extending to Burns Monument. Operation ceased in 1931. The front exit can be seen under the stairs of double-decker No 22, which had started life in 1913 with an open top deck.

RR'S
WATERS.
HUDSONS

CHAMPIONSHIP BEER
GREAT BRITAIN
TOWNHILL
CHOCOLATES
LOCHORE
20

Far left: The 4ft gauge Falkirk trams served a circular route some six miles round. This is one of the original French-built cars of 1905. **Left:** Two typical open toppers on the 3ft 6in gauge Dunfermline and District Tramways. **Bottom left:** Of 1900 vintage, No 15 of the Dundee, Broughty Ferry and District Tramways initially had an open top deck and was acquired from neighbouring Dundee Corporation for the route to Monifieth; it was replaced by buses in 1931.

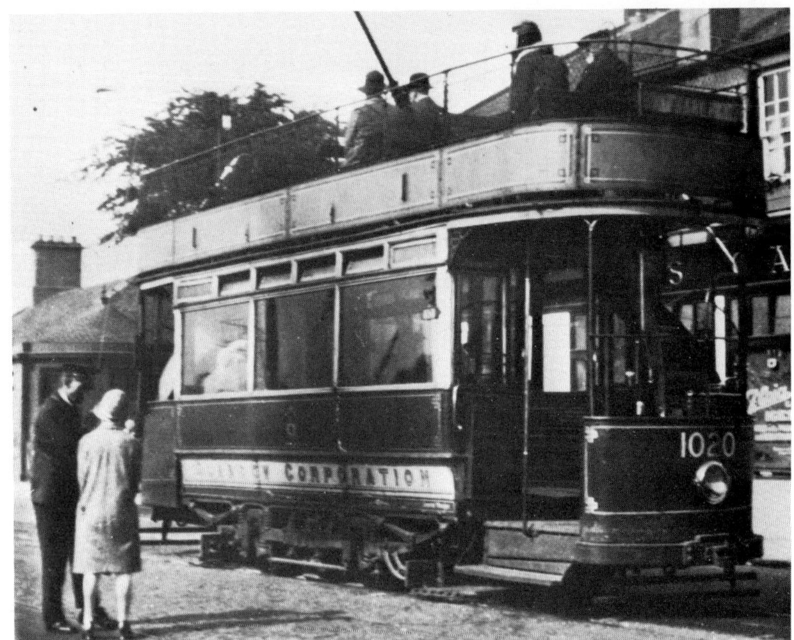

Two glimpses of Glasgow before the great modernisation of 1928-30. **Above:** No 1020, an ex-Paisley car of 1904, was taken over by Glasgow Corporation in 1923. Many of the type were cut down to single-deck, but No 1020 still retained its open top deck when seen here at work on the Kilbarchan route. **Left:** Glasgow No 602 was a characteristic Glasgow-built standard car of 1901-2, at first with open top but later covered. During 1928-30 these cars were given fully-enclosed top decks, high-speed motors and other improvements. The Glasgow tramways, on the 4ft 7¾in gauge, formed the largest system in Scotland, with a fleet of over 1,000 cars on some 150 miles of routes.

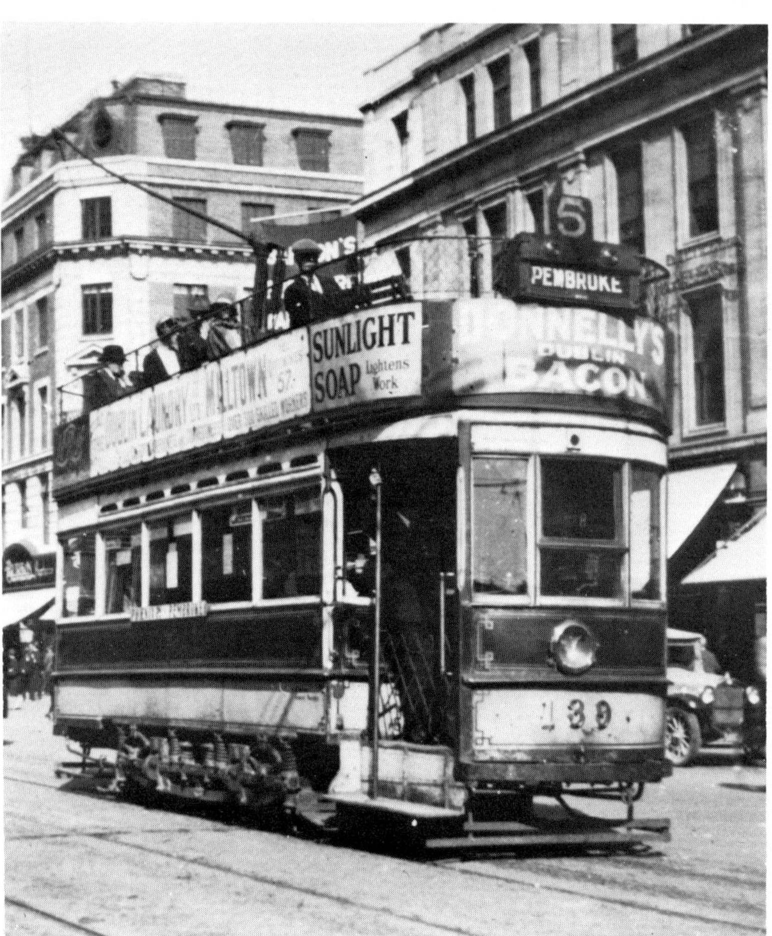

Ireland

Above: The centre of the Dublin system was O'Connell Street, with four parallel tracks where many services terminated at Nelson Pillar. Enclosed ends were an early feature, while open-top cars were retained only for routes with low bridges. **Left:** On open topper No 189 note the two lenses in the destination box; these showed coloured lights to indicate the route before numbers were introduced. **Right:** Balcony-top and fully-enclosed cars, the latter showing the characteristic roof curve above the windscreen. The fleet consisted largely of four wheelers of the Dublin United Tramways Company's own construction.

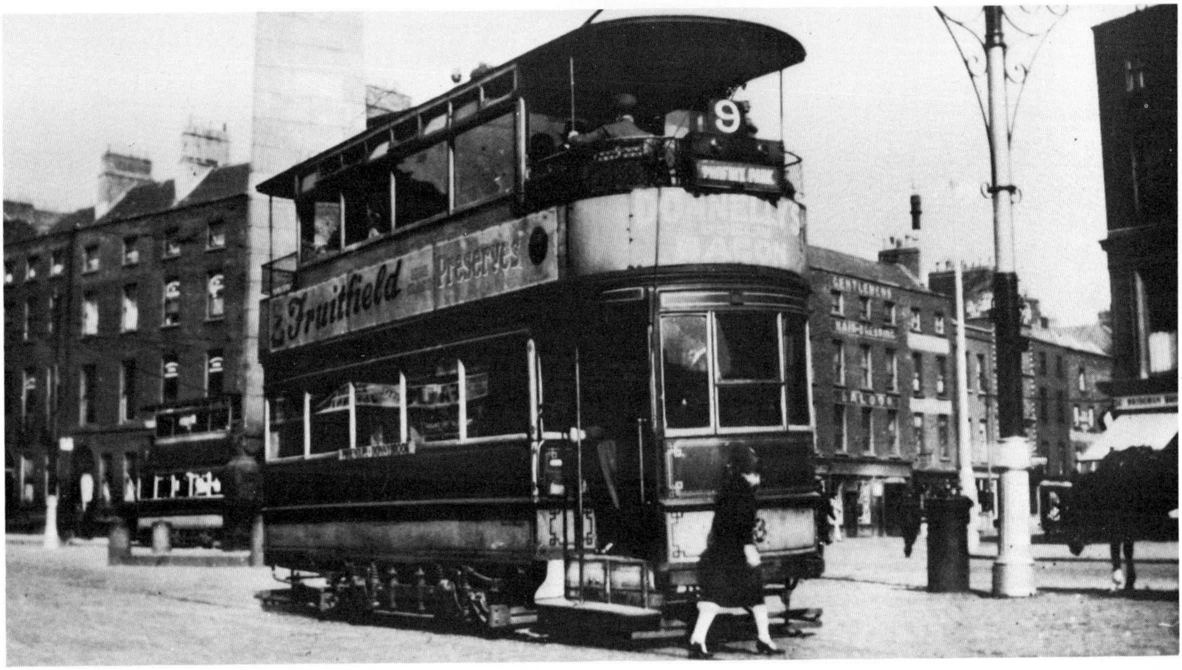
9
Fruitfield
Preserves

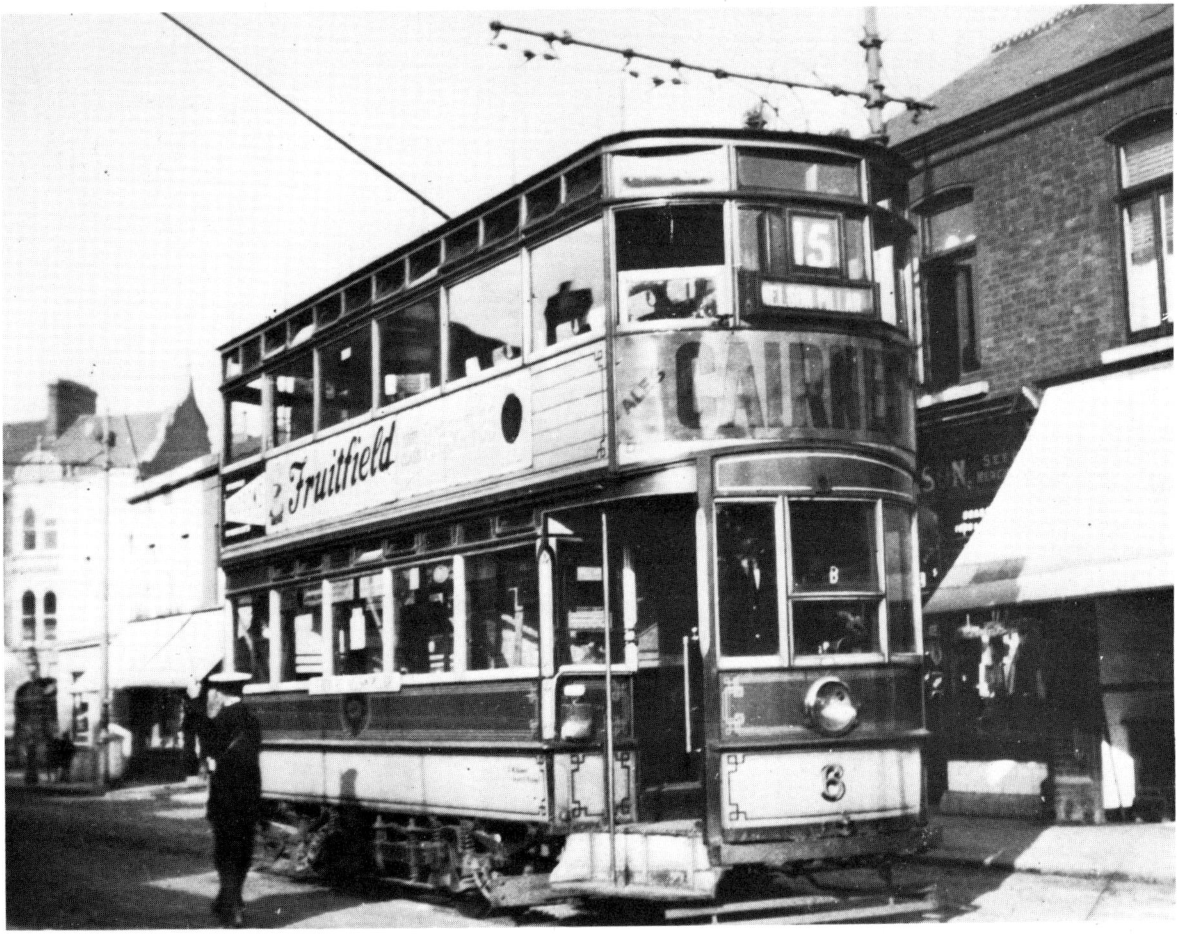
15
Fruitfield
8

Glimpsed in their depot **(right)** the 5ft 3in gauge Dublin cars make an interesting contrast with those of Belfast Corporation **(below)**, the only tramway system in Ireland to use the standard 4ft 8½in gauge. Early open-top cars were progressively rebuilt with top covers; notable are the deep windows in the short enclosed top of this one.

To the Continent

A bleak day on the seafront in Guernsey **(left)**, where the three-mile electric line ran between St Peter Port and St Sampsons until 1934. Opened with steam traction, it became one of the earliest electric tramways in 1892. A quiet moment on the Boulogne tramways **(below)**, the first Continental system encountered by many British travellers on their arrival at this French port. Electric trams started here in 1898 and the last were in evidence until 1951. The metal route disc can be seen on the dash.

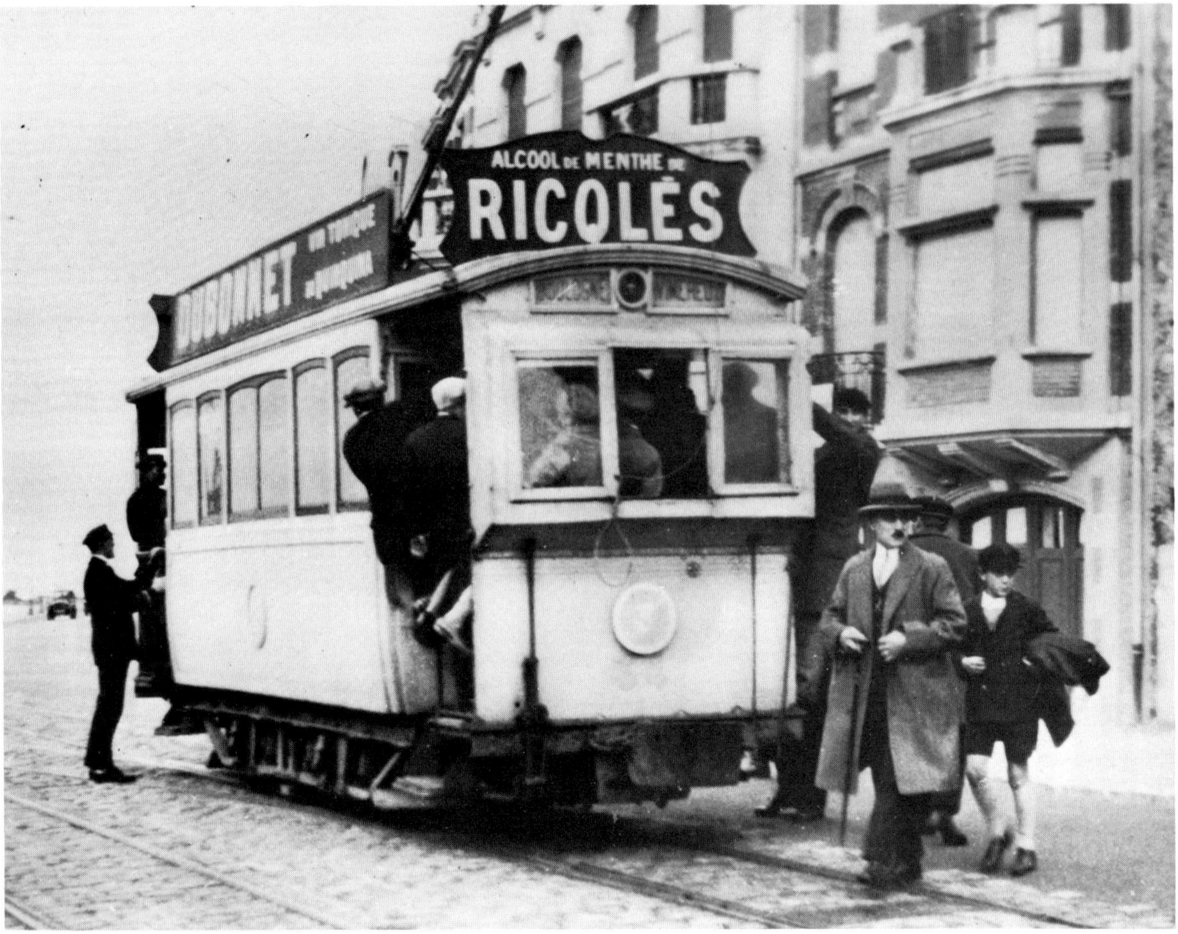
ALCOOL DE MENTHE DE
RICQLÈS
DUBONNET

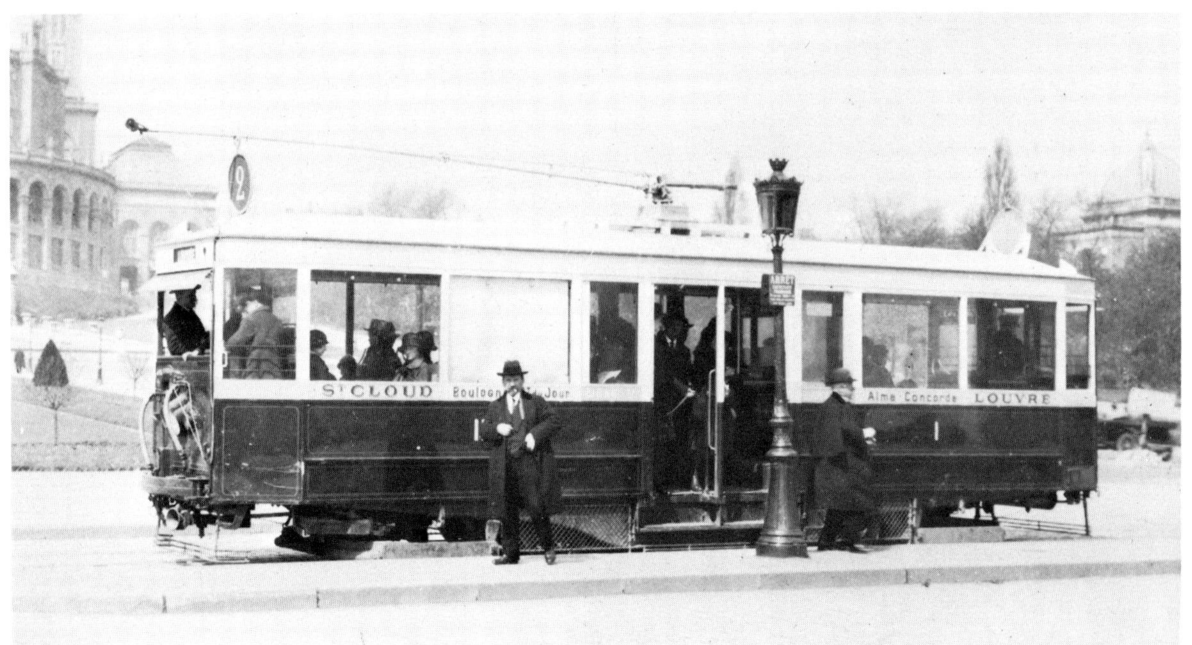

2
St CLOUD
Alma Concorde LOUVRE

Left: Rush hour in Boulogne! Some 30 motor cars served five routes in the town. **Below left:** Inland to Paris, where a typical central-entrance car is at work on the conduit tracks in the central area. Note the trolley pole hooked down. Paris tramways at the end of the 1920s had some 2,500 motor cars and trailers, but the last were withdrawn in 1938. **Top right:** On to Belgium, where electric cars of the Societe Nationale des Chemins de Fer Vicinaux, the 'Vicinal', worked services in the port and resort of Ostend. Here a typical four-wheeler patrols a deserted sea front. The Vicinal's first electric tramway had started in Brussels in 1894, and the company operated lines in numerous Belgian towns. **Centre right:** Also in Ostend were other trams of the Vicinal, providing interurban services both along the coast and inland. At this time, some were still powered by steam, with 0-6-0 locomotives like this; at the peak of steam traction, the Vicinal had some 1,000 locomotives on 3,000 miles of tramways and light railways across the country. Although passenger services by steam were generally withdrawn during the 1930s, some were restored during World War II. **Below:** Brussels opened its first horse tramway as early as 1869, and at the end of the 1920s when this photograph was taken a close mesh of routes served the city and its suburbs. Although much modernisation of the rolling stock took place during the 1930s, four-wheel motor cars and trailers not unlike these were still to be seen until only a few years ago; they have since been displaced by modern cars and the Metro.

Left: Another scene on the Brussels undertaking, with a typical two-car 'train' of motor and trailer characteristic of Continental practice of the period. Note the large tail lamp on the trailer. **Below left:** In Holland Dr Whitcombe found steam trams still functioning in some areas, though many were falling victim to the motor bus. This is a train of the Ooster Steamtram Company; the locomotive was built by Breda in 1885. Note the luggage van.

Above: Another Dutch steam tramway, this time the Betuwsche operating in the Arnhem area; it was replaced by buses in 1933. The engine, dignified with the name *Baron Van Der Feltz*, is again by Breda; the driver's position at the controls can be seen, as well as the warning bell. **Centre left:** The North-South Holland Tramway Company (NZH) possessed a network of both metre gauge and standard gauge lines, connecting Amsterdam, Haarlem, Leiden and The Hague, as well as the coastal towns of Zandvoort, Noordwijk and Katwijk; the last of them continued until 1961. Here is electric car No 50 at the terminus of a Haarlem local service at Bloemendaal; the 'destination board' proclaims it as a one-man operated car. **Bottom left:** In Groningen, the northernmost town system in the Netherlands. The first horse trams here began in 1880 and electrification came in 1910; operation ceased in 1949.

Top right: A German interurban tramway; a train on the Köln-Bonner Eisenbahn connecting Cologne and Bonn, running on the urban tracks at each end of the route but on its own right of way between. The line originated in a steam tramway in 1898 and still runs, though with more modern rolling stock than these massive central-entrance cars. **Centre right:** A three-car train on the Cologne city service; again, as in many German cities, the tramways continue to function, having been upgraded with new rolling stock and with subways in the congested central areas. Cologne's first horse tramway started in 1877 and the first electric line in 1901. **Below:** Munich's library tram was an innovation when this photograph was taken, but it was to become an established institution and the vehicle is now preserved as a museum piece.

Tailpiece – A 50 year Contrast

Half a century's progress in the tramcar is epitomised in these two London vehicles: a horse tram of the 1880s and a 'Pullman' tram of 1930.

Bibliography

Those who wish to supplement the photographs in the present volume by seeking more about the history of tramways in general will find that the following books provide a useful basis as well as a starting point for further study.

History of Tramways; R. A. Buckley; David and Charles, 1975. An outline of world tramway history.

Buses, Trolleys and Trams; Charles S. Dunbar; Paul Hamlyn, 1967. A popular history, world-wide in coverage.

The Golden Age of Tramways; Charles F. Klapper; Routledge and Kegan Paul, 1961. A detailed and meticulous history.

Great British Tramway Networks; W. H. Bett and J. C. Gillham; Light Railway Transport League, 4th Edition 1962, and now being issued in revised geographical parts, edited by J. H. Price. Comprehensive topographical and historical details of all British tramways.

Tramway Heyday; J. Joyce; Ian Allan, 1964. A history of British tramways in their social context.

Tramways of the World; J. Joyce; Ian Allan, 1965. Some of the great tramway systems of the world, past and present.

Dr H. A. Whitcombe; 'History of the Steam Tram' was a paper read before the Institution of Locomotive Engineers in London on 6 January 1937, and printed as Paper No 367 in the *Journal of the Institution of Locomotive Engineers*. A new edition, edited and with an introduction by Charles E. Lee, was published by the Oakwood Press in 1954.